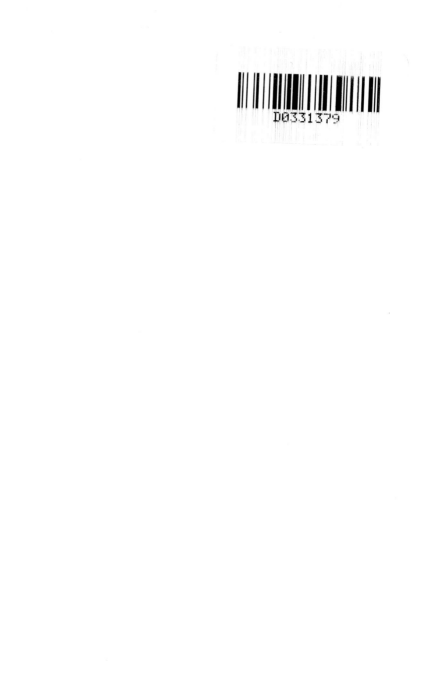

EDITION

Devotional Thoughts for SPORTS FANS of
Baseball, Basketball, Football, and Hockey

DAVE BRANON, EDITOR

DISCOVERY HOUSE
PUBLISHERS®

Feeding the Soul with the Word of God

Discovery House Publishers is affiliated with RBC Ministries,
Grand Rapids, Michigan.

Discovery House books are distributed to the trade exclusively by
Barbour Publishing, Inc., Uhrichsville, Ohio.

Requests for permission to quote from this book should be directed to:
Permissions Department, Discovery House Publishers,
P.O. Box 3566,Grand Rapids, MI 49501,
or contact us by e-mail at permissionsdept@dhp.org.

All Scripture quotations, unless otherwise indicated, are taken from the
Holy Bible, New International Version®, NIV®. Copyright ©1973,
1978, 1984 by Biblica, Inc.™ Used by permission of Zondervan.
All rights reserved worldwide. www.zondervan.com.

Interior design by Sherri L. Hoffman
Cover design by Steve Gier

ISBN: 978-1-57293-457-3

Printed in the United States of America

11 12 13 14 / 10 9 8 7 6 5 4 3 2 1

CONTENTS

Introduction 7
100 Great Games In Sports History . . 11

HOCKEY

1. Hanging Out with Gretzky 14
2. Hockey, Pistol Pete, and Heaven . . 16
3. My Two Front Teeth 18
4. A Wilderness Adventure 20
5. "Is That a Girl Playing Hockey?" . . 22
6. More Important Than the Cup! . . . 24
7. From Nightmare to Dream 26
8. The Greatest Goal 28
9. A Temporary Job 30
10. Three Ordinary Guys 32
11. Afraid? 34
12. How Holly Met Bob 36
13. Got You Covered 38
14. In the Middle of a Struggle 40
15. "Dear Dominic" 42
16. Think Fast! 44
17. Too Young? 46
18. Turned Away 48
19. Captain Coyote 50
20. Remarkable Forgiveness 52
21. We're All Goalies 54
22. Create a Monument 56
23. Zach and the Kid 58
24. The Apprentice 60
25. Keep an Eye on Him! 62

BASKETBALL

26. Seek Wisdom and
    Understanding 64

27. Not-So-Fundamental 66
28. The Shot That Made
    March Mad 68
29. Pistol Pete's Search 70
30. Five Superstars 72
31. Stand Tall 74
32. What's Your Focal Point? 76
33. The Bond of Basketball—and
    Beyond 78
34. Sign Me Up! 80
35. Cooler Heads 82
36. Not Enough 84
37. Steve Nash's Ego 86
38. Driving a Different Lane 88
39. Original Rules for Sale 90
40. The Great Jimmy V. 92
41. Setting Up Some Expectations . . . 94
42. J Will's Deferred Dream 96
43. Playing Like the Pistol 98
44. Getting Fit 100
45. The Best Legacy 102
46. Lessons from the Waterboys . . . 104
47. No Pain, No Gain 106
48. Jimmy Chitwood's Jumper 108
49. Game-Clock Math 110
50. Be an Example 112

BASEBALL

51. The Legacy of Ernie Harwell . . . 114
52. Take Me Out to the Ball Game . . 116
53. Are You Optimistic? 118
54. What Will the Outcome Be? . . . 120
55. My Awful Week 122

56. As If It Never Happened 124
57. Moses, Hope, and the
    Chicago Cubs 126
58. Take Time to Rest 128
59. What Big Mac Lacks 130
60. Extra Boost? 132
61. Don't Imitate Him 134
62. A Legacy of Resilience 136
63. The Complain Game 138
64. In a Slump? 140
65. Curses! 142
66. A Proud Father 144
67. Forgive and Remember 146
68. Cutting Out Shortcuts 148
69. What My Player Can Do 150
70. What Pete Rose Can't Get 152
71. Cutting Some Slack 154
72. The Power of Example 156
73. Come On, Ump! 158
74. Do the Right Thing 160
75. Sweeney's Surrender 162

FOOTBALL

76. You're Not Tim Tebow! 164
77. You Do What on Sunday? 166
78. One Single Fan 168
79. Only Way to Turn 170

80. Why Walk Away? 172
81. He Kept Going and Going 174
82. Going the Right Way? 176
83. Say No to Immorality 178
84. Lasting Satisfaction? 180
85. Encouragement and
    Instruction 182
86. The Right Role Model 184
87. Be Like Mike . . . Brown 186
88. Take One for the Team 188
89. A Fresh Start 190
90. A Humbling Experience 192
91. Double Coverage Trouble 194
92. Leon's Lapse 196
93. Tender Macho Man 198
94. A Great Loss 200
95. Kids' Stuff 202
96. A 280-Pound Puppy Dog 204
97. What Really Lasts 206
98. Stick to It 208
99. Decisions, Decisions 210
100. We Are Family 212

Key Verse List 214
Sports People 217
Power Up Writers 219
Note to the Reader 222

INTRODUCTION

The Big Four, they call them. Four major team sports in North America—the ones that have the longest tradition and the biggest following. Hockey. Basketball. Baseball. Football.

They are the ones with the famous North American championships: The Stanley Cup. The Final Four. The NBA Finals. The World Series. The BCS Championship. The Super Bowl. Each year the total attendance at NHL, Major League Baseball, NBA, NFL, and NCAA basketball and football games equals two-thirds of the population of the United States. In 2009, 196,517,983 tickets were purchased for the four major men's team sports and for college football and basketball. That's a lot of spectating. And that doesn't even touch the number of folks who watched the games in the cozy convenience of their living rooms.

Add to that the millions of young people who play these sports, and it all computes to huge interest in slapshots, home runs, jump shots, and touchdowns.

Consider for a moment that there is hardly a day that goes by in North America where one of these sports is not competed on a national level—and on many days several different sports are in session at once. And yet fans can't seem to get enough.

The baseball season gets underway during college basketball's March Madness for both the men and the women. And soon after the last Shining Moment occurs on the college courts, the NHL and NBA begin their playoffs.

Baseball soldiers on while the guys in the shorts and the guys in the jerseys work their way to their finals in June. A typical example was in early June 2010 when Game 3 of the

NBA Finals tipped off in Boston between the Celtics and the Los Angeles Lakers just minutes after Stephen Strasburg finished his major league debut for the Washington Nationals by striking out 14 batters—the last seven in a row. That's the kind of sports overlap that keeps a true sports fan happy.

Along the way as baseball heats up and hockey and basketball wind down, the WNBA tips off for its summer of hoops.

For one brief period after the NBA and NHL crown their champions in June, baseball is king again. Then the NBA holds its draft, the NFL training camps start, and fans start looking forward to fall. The major league All-Star game alerts baseball fans that the season is about half over, and it isn't long until football fever breaks out.

As the pennant races march toward October, college football and pro football kick off and take over again as the ruling sport. The baseball playoffs pick up steam toward the World Series, and just as they gain momentum, it's time for the NHL to face off again.

The NFL and the NCAA plow ahead into an increasingly crowded schedule as NBA training camps open—and everybody's playing again.

Finally, the World Series ends, and the NFL begins its second half. College football races headlong toward the bowl games, and the NBA and NHL plug along.

Christmas time means an increased interest in the gridiron as the top teams jockey for a chance at championships. The BCS gets the first part of January's attention as the bowl games are contested and the collegiate champion is crowned. Then the NFL takes center stage for the Super Bowl—the biggest team sporting event of the year.

The end of that game signals an uptick in college basketball attention as the smell of March wafts through the air. The boys of summer begin to limber up, fans across the land fill in their March Madness brackets, the college skaters head for the Frozen Four, and it's soon time for the whole thing to start over.

We can learn a lot by watching these four major team sports throughout the year. We learn about sportsmanship when an umpire destroys a perfect game and apologizes to a pitcher who handles it all with grace. We learn about living with class and dignity when we study the lives of remarkable men such as John Wooden, Ernie Harwell, Eddie Robinson, Jim Valvano, and others who have come and gone. We learn about perseverance as we watch players like Jamie Moyer, Brett Favre, Grant Hill, and Chris Chelios battle injuries and advancing age to perform with excellence. We learn about leadership as we see Derek Fisher, Rajon Rondo, Drew Brees, Sid Crosby, Derek Jeter, and others like them carry teams along with the power of their personalities and the example of their professionalism.

And we can look at what happens in the world of team sports and learn a lot about the spiritual side of life. The stories that come out of the games people play can often illustrate biblical truth. That's what the writers of *Power Up! All-Star Edition* were looking for. As either observers of these sports that fill in our sports calendars or actual participants in these contests, the writers have looked for and discovered lessons that have scriptural roots.

That allows us the luxury of reading even more about the sports we enjoy while learning how better to serve, honor, and worship the God we love. So put the TV on mute as you watch that NBA game, turn down the sound on your laptop as you catch a game on MLB-TV, or set aside your fantasy football stats for a few minutes so you can catch all the action and all the challenges of *Power Up! All-Star Edition.*

Like team sports in North America, you can enjoy this book year-round and never tire of what it offers you.

DAVE BRANON, EDITOR
Power Up! All-Star Edition

100 GREAT GAMES IN SPORTS HISTORY

What does it take to make a game great?

Many years ago, I was watching a major league baseball game as the pitcher mowed down hitter after hitter—until he had retired 26 batters in a row. As I watched, I grew more nervous and more excited the closer he got to the last out. With two outs in the ninth, as I was pacing the room and trying to catch my breath, the 27th hitter lined a solid single into the outfield and broke up the perfect game. As nearly flawless as that game was, it is not even considered for a spot in the pantheon of greatness. You would have to look long and hard to find a reference to it in baseball history. One base hit made it rather ordinary.

Then, while compiling this book, I was watching again as another pitcher edged toward perfection. Detroit's Armando Galarraga got the first 26 Cleveland Indians out—and then came a play baseball fans will never forget. Cleveland's Jason Donald grounded a ball to the right side. Miguel Cabrera fielded it, and he threw to Galarraga covering first. As I watched, I saw Galarraga catch the ball and put his foot on the bag before Donald reached first. I knew I had just witnessed a perfect game.

But before the first celebratory word could escape my lips, a shocking scene unfolded. The first base umpire spread his hands out to indicate that Donald was safe.

Just as had happened all those years previous, a single had ruined a perfect game.

Yet because of the circumstances of this game, it will live on in baseball history as one of the greatest ever played. It will long be remembered and talked about. In a scorebook, both games look exactly alike up till that point: 26 outs and a single. But they were far from the same.

Galarraga's game erupted into a national firestorm of protest as fans across the country were tuned in to see the error of umpire Jim Joyce's ways. He had erred in his safe call, and everyone knew it. When he discovered what he had done, even this hardened umpire was crushed. "I just cost that kid a perfect game," he would say in dismay later that night.

And through it all, Armando Galarraga displayed more courage and maturity than fans had observed in a long time from one young athlete.

One ground ball. One blown call. One amazingly grace-filled reaction from a young pitcher. And you have the formula for greatness. The game may not have been recorded as a perfect game, but it was indeed great.

Great games in sports sometimes sneak up on you. Like in a hockey game in which a team has a three-goal lead late in the game. But a goal here, a goal there, and suddenly there's a historical comeback on the horizon.

Some games have a greatness edge because of the circumstances—such as a seventh game of the Stanley Cup or the World Series or the NBA Finals. Or the Super Bowl. But the game is not great without heroics or tension or some kind of outstanding play.

Sometimes one individual can make a game great. Wilt Chamberlain's 100-point NBA performance in 1962 is perhaps the most outstanding such example.

Sometimes it takes a team to make it happen, as with Villanova in the 1985 NCAA men's basketball championship game. Rollie Massimino's kids shot over 78 percent to topple top-ranked Georgetown. Who knew that would happen?

As we considered what games to include in these four lists of 25 great games, one thing we didn't want to do was to try to quantify the games as the Top 100 Greatest Games Ever. That might make for good arguments, but it's nearly an impossible task. So we simply chose 25 great games from each of the four sports covered in *Power Up! All-Star Edition*. Some are long-ago games that may have been largely forgotten. Some are of more recent vintage. The goal was to give true sports fans a glimpse of the wide variety of ways greatness can occur in the world of sports.

If your favorite game of all time isn't on one of the lists, it doesn't mean we didn't think it was great—it simply means we ran out of room to mention them all. We hope the list gives you some good memories of some of the most outstanding games ever played.

—DAVE BRANON

1. HANGING OUT WITH GRETZKY

Game Plan:
Keeping the big picture in mind

"The body is a unit, though it is made up of many parts."
1 CORINTHIANS 12:12

During my 20-year pro hockey career, I had the honor of representing my country in international competition several times. When the best of the best come together to see who the dominant country in hockey is, you know how important that is to Canada. When you're from my country (I was born in Ottawa, Ontario), there's only one medal that counts: Gold.

In 1987, the Canada Cup tournament, the precursor to the World Cup, was about to be contested, and I was selected to try out for the team. After just coming off a successful campaign with the Washington Capitals, I was looking forward to making the team and having a big offensive impact on Canadian success.

FAST FACT:
Mike Gartner, who scored 708 goals during his career from 1979 through 1998, was elected to the Hockey Hall of Fame in 2001.

Things turned out a little different from what I planned.

I had a good training camp, but as I looked around the dressing room and saw players such as Wayne Gretzky, Mario Lemieux, and Mark Messier, I wondered how I was going to make the team. If I didn't change what I brought to the table, I figured, I probably wouldn't make it.

So I decided to become a checker and penalty killer. I was a goal scorer up to that point in my career, but on this team we had an abundance of those. So I thought my only chance of getting to play in the Canada Cup this time around would be to adapt to what the team needed, take on a lesser role, and see what happens.

As it turned out, we won the Cup by beating Russia 6-5 in the finals. Each of the three final-round games ended with that score. Russia won Game 1, and Canada won the last two to capture the Cup.

I learned a valuable lesson about being a smaller part of a bigger picture. Isn't that what Paul was talking about in his letter to the Corinthian church? As Christians we are all parts, great or small, of the larger body. Everything we do—big or little—should be done for the greater goal: For God's glory.

—MIKE GARTNER

FOLLOW THROUGH

Are you dealing right now with a role that is smaller than what you had envisioned for yourself? Talk it over with God, and ask Him to help you see the value you have for the team.

From the Playbook: Read 1 Corinthians 12.

GREAT HOCKEY GAMES

6-5 TIMES THREE **September 11, 1987 Canada 6, Russia 5**— Fifteen years after Canada beat Russia in the Summit Series (See devotional No. 8), they went at it again—this time in the Canada Cup finals. In this best-of-three series, each game ended with the same score: 6-5. Russia won Game 1. Canada; Game 2. After Russia jumped out to a 3-0 lead in Game 3, the Canadians came back to lead 5-4. After Russia tied it up, two of the game's biggest stars took over. With just over a minute left, Mario Lemieux teamed up with Wayne Gretzky for a Lemieux gamewinner.

2. HOCKEY, PISTOL PETE, AND HEAVEN

Game Plan:
Making sure of your salvation

"Man is destined to die once, and after that to face judgment." HEBREWS 9:27

There's a guy in Peterborough, Ontario, who loves—and lives for—hockey.

In the basement of his home, John Townsend created a replica of the center line in the arena where his beloved Toronto Maple Leafs play. Pennants hang from the ceiling and hockey cards adorn the walls. It's where Townsend and his hockey-loving buddies watch the games on TV. He even told a reporter, "I want to die in this room."

I guess if you have to go—and if you had a choice—you may as well check out in a place you'd like to be and doing what you enjoy.

Personally, I think I'd favor going as Pistol Pete Maravich went. The greatest scorer in Division I college basketball history—and my all-time favorite athlete—died at age 40 while playing pick-up basketball.

Death isn't something we like to think about. Who wants to spend valuable time seriously considering the idea of dying? But we can't avoid it. And to be abundantly clear about this subject, the most important issue is not where you are when you die, but where you're going after you die.

When Maravich breathed his last breath on January 5, 1988, it didn't matter to him if he had been playing basketball

FAST FACT:

Pete Maravich, playing before the three-point line had been implemented, scored 3,667 points and averaged 44.2 points a game. It has been estimated that with the three-point line, he would have averaged 57 points a game.

in a gym in California or washing dishes at home in Louisiana. What mattered was that He had put his faith in Jesus Christ. Because he was a Christian, when Pete died he went right into heaven to be with the Lord he loved.

Death takes everyone; that's the bad news. But there's good news: Trusting Jesus makes the prospects of life here on earth a lot brighter, and it guarantees a life in heaven in the presence of God.

Heaven is reserved for everyone who trusts in Jesus. Have you put your faith in Him as your Savior? No matter where you are when your time on earth ends, do you know that you are headed for heaven?   —DAVE BRANON

FOLLOW THROUGH

Are you ready to cross that threshold between earth and heaven? If not, is there someone you should talk to about this so you can be sure? Read John 3 for help in learning about faith in Christ.

From the Playbook: Read 2 Corinthians 5:1–9.

TOP 25 GREAT HOCKEY GAMES

THE GREAT ONE'S GREATEST May 29, 1993, LA Kings 5, Toronto Maple Leafs 4—Some consider the seventh game of the 1993 Campbell Conference finals the greatest game Wayne Gretzky ever played. In the contest, he willed his way to a hat trick (a rare seventh-game occurrence) and an assist—and with the force of his will led the LA Kings past the favored Toronto Maple Leafs 5-4 and into the Stanley Cup Finals. For the first time, the LA Kings would go that far in Stanley Cup play. Gretzky himself has called this the best game of his wonderful career. The Kings lost to Montreal in the Stanley Cup Finals.

3. MY TWO FRONT TEETH

Game Plan:
Staying safe spiritually

"Put on the full armor of God." EPHESIANS 6:13

As an athlete, I put on my protective equipment every time I go on the ice. From shin guards to elbow pads to helmets, every piece serves a purpose. A few years ago, I learned the hard way that there are no spare parts when it comes to playing it safe.

At the end of practice one day, there were just two of us players left out on the ice. I removed my mouth guard to speak with the equipment manager. Just as I did, my teammate fired off one last slap shot. You can guess what happened. His shot deflected off the cross bar on the goal and ricocheted right toward me. The puck smacked me square in the mouth, knocking out my two front teeth.

FAST FACT:
According to Shane Doan, he has lost three teeth in his hockey career. Not bad for well over 1,000 games.

I was not at all pleased. My teeth had survived almost 20 years of hockey since I first laced on skates as a small boy. Now I had to endure countless dental appointments, root canals, even false teeth—all because I let down my guard for just one moment, leaving me without the proper equipment to protect my teeth.

As believers in Jesus Christ, we need to be clothed daily in the protective equipment that He offers us—such as the belt of truth, the shield of faith, and the helmet of salvation to name just a few. This armor of God protects our hearts and minds from danger, just as sports equipment protects our body. And every piece of this godly armor is vital. If we neglect even a seemingly small area of our lives, we can leave ourselves open to damage that will hinder our walk with God.

Study the armor of God that Paul describes for us in Ephesians 6:12–17. Put on your protection every day. Be smart, and remember that there are no spare parts. That way you won't get your teeth knocked out. —SHANE DOAN

FOLLOW THROUGH

Can you think of a specific example where you let down your guard and allowed something to hinder your walk with God? Can you identify the piece of God's armor that would have protected you in that situation? What things can you do to "put on the full armor of God"?

From the Playbook: Read Ephesians 6:13–17.

MONDAY NIGHT MIRACLE May 12, 1986, St. Louis Blues 6, Calgary Flames 5—Game 6 of the Campbell Conference finals. The Calgary Flames had scorched their way to a 5-2 lead with just 12 minutes left in their game with the St. Louis Blues. The home crowd at the St. Louis Arena was not expecting much until Brian Sutter poked in a goal after the puck deflected off Flames' goalie Mike Vernon. Now, with eight minutes to go, the lead had shrunk to 5-3. Greg Paslawski scored, but with less than two minutes left, it was still 5-4 Calgary. With just a minute left, Paslawski struck again—and the arena erupted. In OT, Doug Wickenheiser completed the miracle with a game-winning shot.

4. A WILDERNESS ADVENTURE

"Great are the works of the Lord; they are pondered by all who delight in them." Psalm 111:2

Where does a professional hockey player go to escape after a long, extended hockey season? Where can he be free from cell phones, e-mails, and the constant demands of press and public?

North to Alaska!

At least that's where Ottawa Senators center Mike Fisher went after the 2005–06 NHL season—long before he met and married Carrie Underwood.

Mike Fisher's excellent wilderness adventure took him to the pristine wilds of Alaska for a week in August.

FAST FACT:
During the off-season, Mike Fisher conducts hockey camps with Hockey Ministries International.

Mike, his brother Bud, cousin Warren, and former big-league reliever Tim Burke took flight and landed where nobody could reach them.

Burke, who serves with Hockey Ministries International helping to coordinate that ministry's NHL chapel program, had been to Alaska before and shared his experiences with Mike.

Fisher got in touch with Rocky, their wilderness guide, and arrangements were made for their summer escape.

The guys were "fully aware that they were in the midst of God's incredible creation," as Fisher describes it. Burke says that being with three other Christian guys created a "unique dynamic of being in the middle of nowhere where you couldn't get a message to anyone if you wanted to. The environment breeds bonding." Sharing space with moose, bear, and bald eagles while hooking more than enough silver salmon and northern pike was, they say, an unforgettable experience.

The increased awareness of God's majesty added a spiritual edge that won't soon be forgotten.

Mike and the boys say that they returned with a greater appreciation than ever of God's mighty power and the strength derived when godly guys get together.

Sometimes it takes being immersed in God's great creation to refocus us on the Creator himself. Can you work it out so that you can get away from everything electronic, everything artificial, everything culturally relevant to bask in the greatness of the Lord's majestic work? It might be just what you need to draw closer to God.   —DAVID FISHER

FOLLOW THROUGH

What would be the benefit of a little "out in creation" time for you? What do you think would change for you if you had a retreat as Mike experienced?

From the Playbook: Read Psalm 19:1–7.

GREAT HOCKEY GAMES

END OF A DROUGHT **June 14, 1994, New York Rangers 3, Vancouver Canucks 2**—Madison Square Garden. Home of so many great sporting events. But it had never been the site of a Rangers' Stanley Cup victory championship. And the last time the Rangers had won the Cup was 1940. Game 7 against the Vancouver Canucks was everything everyone hoped it would be. The Rangers jumped out to a 2-0 lead in the first stanza. Vancouver halved the lead, but Mark Messier made it 3-1. Early in the third, Trevor Linden scored his second goal, but New York held on to win 3-2.

5. "IS THAT A GIRL PLAYING HOCKEY?"

Game Plan:
Stepping up for God

"Man looks at the outward appearance, but the Lord looks at the heart." 1 SAMUEL 16:7

When 9-year-old Abby Hoffman decided she wanted to play hockey in her hometown during the mid-1950s, her parents realized that there were no leagues for girls in the Toronto area. So the innovative Hoffmans cut their daughter's hair and registered her as "Ab Hoffman" in the only league available—a boys' league. Ab was selected for the Toronto Hockey League All-Star team. But when Ab produced the required birth certificate, league officials were shocked to discover that Ab was really "Abigail." She was dismissed from the team, and the story made international news.

FAST FACT:
Abby Hoffman represented Canada in the Olympics four times in athletics, running the 400- and 800-meter events.

Many years later, after representing Canada at four Olympic tournaments, Abby Hoffman assisted the Canadian Amateur Hockey Association in implementing a national women's hockey championship. Today, representatives from each province vie for the "Abby Hoffman Trophy."

She was part of the movement that led Canadian women's hockey to be the best in the world—including winning the 2010 Olympic Winter Games gold medal in Vancouver. Abby may not have looked "the part" in the beginning, but she was instrumental in breaking down barriers for women in the sport of hockey.

Scripture records the name of another young person who didn't look the part. His name was David. Not able to fit into the coat of armor or the bronze helmet of a warrior, David used five small stones and a sling to conquer a 9-foot-tall Philistine named Goliath.

Earlier, the youngest son of Jesse had been summoned from tending the flocks of sheep to be anointed future king over all of Israel. The story may not have made international news that day, but David was instrumental in breaking down the barriers of the Philistines, as well as becoming a man about whom God said, "I have found … a man after my own heart" (Acts 13:22).

Sometimes we may not "look the part," but if God has called us to do a task, He will also provide us with the strength we need to get the job done. —MOLLY RAMSEYER

FOLLOW THROUGH

Are you too focused on how things appear? What steps can you take today to improve your heart's attitude instead of improving how you look? Remember, appearance doesn't reveal true value!

From the Playbook: Read 1 Samuel 16 and 17.

TOP 25 GREAT HOCKEY GAMES

CANADIAN LADIES' FIRST February 21, 2002, Canada 3, United States 2—When the Olympics first allowed women's hockey to be part of the fun, the United States beat Canada at their own game in 1998. In the Nagano Games, the US ladies won all of their games, including a 3-1 win over Canada in the gold medal battle. Heading into the next Olympics, it appeared that there would be more of the same. In eight contests between Canada and the US as the teams prepared for the Games in Salt Lake City, America won them all. But Canada was improving. The neighbors faced each other in the gold medal game again, but this time Canada won 3-2 for its first Olympic gold in women's hockey.

6. MORE IMPORTANT THAN THE CUP!

"Seeing Jesus, he fell at his feet." MARK 5:22

It finally happened for Glen Wesley.

After playing in more than 150 NHL playoff games, the Carolina Hurricanes' veteran defensemen finally earned the right to hoist Lord Stanley's Cup over his head after his Hurricanes knocked off the Edmonton Oilers in the 2006 Stanley Cup Finals.

The former first-round draft choice of the Boston Bruins had held the distinction of having played the most playoff games of any player in NHL history without ever winning the Cup. He had begun his professional hockey career in 1983 with Portland of the old World Hockey League, moved to the NHL in 1987, and spent the next 19 seasons pursuing hockey's most hallowed trophy.

How did this sage old veteran handle the disappointment of not attaining his goal for so long? Wesley did it with eternal perspective.

Prior to the Stanley Cup Finals, Wesley told sportswriter Dave Pond his thoughts on not yet winning the Cup. "My eternal salvation is far more important to me—it's more important to have that eternal security and one day be at the feet of the Lord than to be at the foot of the Cup."

Glen Wesley has a deep understanding of the significance of knowing Jesus Christ. He understands the importance of being in the very presence of God!

FAST FACT: *Glen Wesley's No. 2 jersey was retired by the Carolina Hurricanes on February 19, 2009.*

In Mark 5, we read the story of another man who understood the significance of being in Jesus' presence. Jairus, the synagogue ruler, had heard of the amazing healing powers of Jesus. So he came pleading with Jesus to heal his daughter. When he got near Jesus, Jairus fell to his feet in humility. (To know the end of Jarius' story, read Mark 5:22–24, 35–43.)

Whether we have a life or death concern, or are merely longing to spend time with God, we must never lose sight of the importance of humbling ourselves at the feet of Jesus.

—ROB BENTZ

FOLLOW THROUGH

Take a position of submission on the floor, bowing at the feet of Jesus. Communicate your love and amazement of His grace and love for you through prayer.

From the Playbook: Read Mark 5:22–24 and 35–43.

GREAT HOCKEY GAMES

ISLANDERS IN A STORM   April 18, 1987, New York Islanders 3, Washington Capitals 2—It had been a long time since a game had gone as long as this one would. It had been since 1943, in fact. The Washington Capitals and the NY Islanders were tied 3-3 in the Patrick Division semifinals. Late in the game Bryan Trottier saved the Isles by scoring to tie the game at 2-2 and send the contest into extra time. The teams battled fruitlessly for 68 minutes—into the fourth overtime. At just before 2 a.m. Pat LaFontaine touched the twine to give the Isles the win and a date with Philadelphia in the next round.

7. FROM NIGHTMARE TO DREAM

"Delight yourself in the Lord and he will give you the desires of your heart." PSALM 37:4

All my life I wanted to play hockey for Canada. Born in Halkirk, Alberta, I had a desire to represent our flag that was even stronger than my desire to play in the NHL. Professional hockey came first, though, when I was drafted by the Winnipeg Jets in 1995. Because I was only 18 at the time, I was still eligible to play in the World Junior Championship, and I had a good shot at making Team Canada that year. But the Jets had their reasons for not sending me back to Juniors, and I was devastated. I felt that I had been robbed of my big chance to play for Canada.

FAST FACT:

Doan played for the combined Winnipeg Jets/Phoenix Coyotes longer than any other player. He began with the Jets in 1995 and moved with the team to Phoenix the following season.

Fast-forward almost 8 years to the spring of 2003. Because my NHL team, the Phoenix Coyotes, had finished out of the playoffs, I was available for the World Championships. This time I was free to jump at the invitation offered me to join Team Canada. I was blessed with the opportunity to live out my dream while playing with an amazing group of talented athletes. And I was even able to contribute a few points along the way to our capturing the gold medal. Later, I also played for Canada in four World Championships and in the 2006 Olympics.

God may not care about a hockey tournament, but He does care about what matters to His children. Just as I had to learn to wait for the right timing to represent my country in hockey, I still have a lot to learn about waiting on God and understanding His timing. But I have trusted God with all of me, including my hopes and desires. I will continue to trust Him to govern those desires, and I am learning that He truly delights in blessing me, even as I delight in knowing Him.

When it seems that God is asking you to wait, hold on. He knows what He is doing. —SHANE DOAN

FOLLOW THROUGH

Do you recognize any times when God has fulfilled a desire? Is there an unfulfilled desire that you have in your heart today? How much time do you spend focusing on God because of the desire, compared with the time you spend simply wanting to know Him?

From the Playbook: Read Ephesians 1:3–6.

TOP 25 GREAT HOCKEY GAMES

HOME, SWEET HOME February 25, 2010, Canada 2, United States 0—The Canadian women proved their dominance in hockey by capturing their third straight Olympic gold medal. The goalies shone in this one, with Canada's Shannon Szabados stopping all 28 American attempts while the US goaltender, Jessie Vetter, stopped 27 of Canada's 29 shots. The Canadians scored twice in the first period—both goals coming off the stick of Marie-Philip Poulin—and then held on for the win.

8. THE GREATEST GOAL

"We make it our goal to please [the Lord]."

2 CORINTHIANS 5:9

On September 28, 1972, at the Luzhniki Ice Palace in Moscow, Paul Henderson lit the lamp and ignited a firestorm of frenzied fans. During the final seconds of an eight-game Soviet-Canada Summit Series, it was Paul's poke that became the winning goal for the Canadians and caused his countrymen to jump and cheer throughout the land.

Looking back on that moment, he states, "Talk about boyhood dreams—that was the highlight of my 18-year hockey career!" What a thrill that must have been for Henderson—to make the play that decided the game and brought glory to the homeland. This has been considered by many to be the greatest win in Canadian hockey history—even greater than Canada's 2010 gold medal win in the Winter Olympics.

FAST FACT:

After retiring, Henderson spent much of his time working with The Leadership Group, which is affiliated with Campus Crusade for Christ.

Henderson, who was discovered in 2010 to have cancer, will forever be remembered in hockey lore for his mighty score. However, he finds the great goal to be a pale comparison to his top victory.

"Coming to know Jesus Christ as my personal Lord and Savior was truly the pinnacle of my entire life," he says. "Giving Him first place in my life has put everything else in its proper perspective."

So what goals in life light your fire? It's not wrong to have objectives and dreams, but the key is understanding where they fit in to your ultimate purpose in this world.

Paul Henderson knows that purpose. So did the apostle Paul. In 2 Corinthians 5 he said that our goal must be to please God. He also wrote, "We must all appear before the judgment seat of Christ, that each one may receive what is due to him for the things done while in the body, whether good or bad" (v.10).

This solemn truth is a reminder for us today to choose the best goal—living in a way that brings glory to Jesus Christ. Is that your goal?   —TOM FELTEN

FOLLOW THROUGH

Write down three life goals. How do they fit with the ultimate goal of glorifying God?

From the Playbook: Read 2 Corinthians 5:1–10 and Psalm 96.

TOP 25 GREAT HOCKEY GAMES

THE SHOT   **September 28, 1972, Canada 6, Russia 5**—Before Sidney Crosby's goal in the 2010 Olympics, the biggest shot in Canadian hockey history was Paul Henderson's gamewinner in 1972. The debate continues as to which of the two is more important. It was called the Summit Series, and Canada was playing Russia for the championship—in Moscow. The teams had each put together a 3-3-1 record. Things were not going well for the Canadians. One player had been booted out of the game, the coach tossed furniture onto the ice, and the small band of Canadians at the game were screaming, "Let's go home!" Instead, they stayed and climbed back from a 5-3 deficit to tie the game. Then Henderson went to work, scoring on a pass from Phil Esposito to win the game with just 34 seconds left.

9. A TEMPORARY JOB

"I consider everything a loss compared to the surpassing greatness of knowing Christ Jesus my Lord." PHILIPPIANS 3:8

What if your NHL career was merely a stepping-stone for what you really wanted to do with your life? For most athletes who make it to the pinnacle of their sport, the idea that there's something beyond the highest level of competition is hard to imagine.

Unless you're Bob Froese.

FAST FACT:
The William M. Jennings Trophy is an annual award given to the goalkeeper(s) who have played a minimum of 25 games for the team with the fewest goals scored against them during the NHL's regular season.

From 1982 through 1990, Froese lived the life that many young goalies only dream about. For parts of eight seasons, he played between the pipes for the Philadelphia Flyers and the New York Rangers.

But he didn't just play goalie—he excelled! Froese participated in the 1986 NHL All-Star Game, and he teamed with fellow Flyers netminder Darren Jensen to win the William M. Jennings Trophy.

But hockey was not Froese's first love. Since the age of five, he was a follower of Jesus Christ. He loved God! Because of that love, Froese dreamed of serving God in pastoral ministry. Yet because of his on-ice success, his preaching dreams were put on hold.

"With some heavy prodding from the people that were close to me, I chose hockey," says Froese.

Yet today, long after he retired from the NHL in 1990, he is doing what he wanted to do as a young boy. "I am so thankful that God has given me the opportunity—the privilege—to serve Him as a pastor!"

In the Scriptures, the apostle Paul was someone who, after his dramatic conversion, quickly developed a kingdom perspective. He understood that all things pale in comparison with knowing God, walking with Him, and serving the Father's purposes.

What are you doing these days? Is there something God is putting on your heart that He wants you to do for Him? Why not get started now preparing yourself to take that next step?

—ROB BENTZ

FOLLOW THROUGH

Read through the words of the apostle Paul in Philippians 3:7–11. Consider the thing(s) in your life that compete against your love for and knowledge of God. Through prayer, confess this distraction as an idol and seek forgiveness. Then ask God to give you a pure heart for Him and a kingdom perspective.

From the Playbook: Read Philippians 3:7–11.

TOP 25 GREAT HOCKEY GAMES

THE REAL COLD WAR **December 31, 1975, Montreal Canadiens 3, Russia 3**—The Canadians had beaten the powerful Russians three years earlier in the Summit Series, and the Soviets were not happy. So, when they brought their superstars called the Red Army to Montreal to play one of the NHL's top teams, it was war. West vs. East. Capitalism vs. communism. The teams battled to a 3-3 tie in what Montreal's Pete Mahovlich called, "the best hockey game I've ever been associated with."

10. THREE ORDINARY GUYS

Game Plan:
Giving your dreams to God

"You intended to harm me, but God intended it for good."
GENESIS 50:20

When Jean-Guy Talbot took a two-hander at a member of the Junior Canadiens in a 1952 hockey game, the bloody result resembled a scalping. Talbot's target never amounted to much after that assault—not on the ice anyway.

Yet Talbot's victim has hoisted the Stanley Cup a record nine times. He has more wins than any head coach in NHL history (1,244). His name is Scotty Bowman—a member of the Hockey Hall of Fame.

FAST FACT:

Scotty Bowman is the only coach (pro baseball, basketball, football, or hockey) to have won major championships with three different teams.

That injury meant the death of a dream as a player. But it gave rise to another dream as a coach, with fantastic results.

The Bible tells of many ordinary guys who became heroes after their dreams died. Accused of a crime he didn't commit, Joseph the dreamer endured slavery and then imprisonment. Yet he eventually became second in command to Pharaoh and rescued his own family from famine. After letting his brothers in on who he was, Joseph graciously told them, "You intended to harm me [by selling me into slavery], but God intended it for good" (Genesis 50:20).

Moses went from a basket in the Nile to Pharaoh's palace. Then he fled the palace because of a crime he did commit. While tending sheep in the desert for 40 years, his dreams all but evaporated—until he led the greatest escape in history—guiding the Israelites away from slavery in Egypt. Psalm

105:26 says, "[God] sent Moses His servant ... whom He had chosen."

Whom He had chosen! Moses must have felt his life slipping away when he raced off to Midian in disgrace at age 40. But as he discovered at a burning bush at age 80, God's plans are always greater than our dreams.

Are your dreams dying? Give them to God. Then hang on! With the Creator, the ride is usually a wild one.

—Tim Gustafson

FOLLOW THROUGH

Write down a couple of your dreams. How do they line up with the priorities God wants you to have? Do you really trust God with your future?

From the Playbook: Read Psalm 105:16–41.

TOP 25 GREATEST HOCKEY GAMES

HABS KEEP HOPES ALIVE   May 10, 1979, Montreal Canadiens 5, Boston Bruins 4—Scotty Bowman's Montreal Canadiens had won the previous three Stanley Cups. But on this night—the Prince of Wales Conference finals—things didn't look good for a four-peat. The Boston Bruins held a 3-1 lead as the teams went to the second intermission. Montreal managed to tie the score, but Boston made it 4-3. With just over a minute left, Guy Lafleur sent the game into overtime. In OT, Yvon Lambert scored for Montreal, who went on to win the Cup Finals against the New York Rangers.

11. AFRAID?

Game Plan:
Developing healthy fear

"Do not be afraid of those who kill the body."
LUKE 12:4

On March 7, 2010, Pittsburgh Penguins winger Matt Cooke delivered a crushing blow on Marc Savard of the Boston Bruins. Just a moment after Savard had fired a shot on goal— Cooke unloaded! His forearm shiver sent the Bruins' dynamic center crashing to the ice with a severe concussion.

The blow caused Savard to miss nearly two months of action. He also had to pass a pair of neurological exams before he could return to action.

Cooke's shot was scrutinized by the National Hockey League and brought new regulations on hits to the head.

Blows to the head are serious, and certainly a head injury is not to be taken lightly. Serious injuries are a major part of most sports, especially hockey. They're an unspoken part of life for an athlete who puts on a helmet for battle in the NHL or the NFL. Yet there is something far more fearful than a potentially debilitating injury—the reality of an all-powerful living God.

In chapter 12 of Luke's gospel, we read the thought-provoking words of Jesus, "I will show you whom you should fear: Fear him who, after the killing of the body, has the power to throw you into hell. Yes, I tell you, fear him"(v. 5).

A healthy fear of the One who made us, sustains us, and

FAST FACT:

Marc Savard returned to the ice for the Bruins during the Eastern Conference semifinals against the Philadelphia Flyers. He scored one goal and assisted on two others during the seven-game series.

gives us life is crucial for all men. In fact, the book of Proverbs tells us that fear is actually not just something to experience—rather it is a true beginning.

"The fear of the Lord is the beginning of knowledge," says the wise man of Proverbs 1:7. And similarly, the psalmist called the fear of the Lord "the beginning of wisdom" (111:10).

Fear, when it is in submission to the holy, righteous, and just God, is not only appropriate—it's necessary.

—ROB BENTZ

FOLLOW THROUGH

Read and contemplate Proverbs 1:7. Then memorize it.

From the Playbook: Read Luke 12:4–7.

TOP 25 GREAT HOCKEY GAMES

BLACKHAWK RESURRECTION   October 13, 2009, Chicago 6, Calgary 5—The United Center was not a very friendly place for the hometown Blackhawks in the first period of their game with the Calgary Flames. An above-capacity crowd of more than 20,000 people wondered why they had wasted their time and money. At 11:53 of the first, Chicago trailed Calgary 5-0. The Hawks didn't panic. They began chipping away. John Madden salvaged a first-period goal. In the second, Chicago scored three times to make it 5-4. Then, with 4:32 left, Patrick Sharp tied the game. And 26 seconds into the overtime, Brent Seabrook made Chicago the winner 6-5 in the biggest comeback in team history.

12. HOW HOLLY MET BOB

"The angel of the Lord appeared to [Moses] in flames of fire from within a bush." EXODUS 3:2

Bob Bassen enjoyed a respectable career in the NHL, playing for several teams until he retired in 2000. His career on the ice was also marked by an exceptional story of love.

While he was with the Dallas Stars but recuperating from a knee injury, he was sitting near the arena ice one day watching a game when he met a woman who worked in the Stars' office. Her name was Holly Yarbrough.

FAST FACT:

Bob and Holly Bassen live in a northern suburb of Dallas and are active in their children's schools.

They struck up a conversation, then a friendship, and then a romance. They eventually married, and Bob moved on to play his final two years—one in Canada and one in St. Louis.

While the ice played a key part in Bob's life, fire also had its role. It was at a bonfire at his church when he was 12 that he trusted Jesus Christ as his Savior.

On that night, the pastor had preached a message from John 3:16.

Bob tells what happened. "I heard that verse, 'For God so loved the world that he gave his one and only Son, that whoever believes in him shall not perish but have eternal life.' I mean, everybody knows that verse. But when the pastor explained eternal life, I couldn't understand it. But I wanted it. I don't think anyone can really fathom everlasting life, but it sounded good. At that bonfire service I accepted Christ."

On the ice, Bassen found a career and his wife. At the fire, he found eternal life.

Fire and ice were a pretty good combination for Bob. God leads us to himself and to the really important things in life in a variety of ways, doesn't He? Back in the Old Testament days, He used fire to get Moses' attention—and throughout history He used a number of other ways to get folks to listen to Him. It's up to us to look for the ways God is tapping us on the shoulder—then listen for His voice as He calls us wherever we are.

—DAVE BRANON

FOLLOW THROUGH

Have you found the eternal life Bob was talking about? Nothing you can ever do is more important than to trust Jesus and have your sins forgiven.

From the Playbook: Read Exodus 3:1–12.

GREAT HOCKEY GAMES

THE NHL HEADS OUTDOORS **November 22, 2003, Montreal Canadiens 4, Edmonton Oilers 3**—For the first time, the NHL took its regular season outside where hockey started. More than 57,000 fans braved frigid Canadian temperatures as Edmonton hosted Montreal for this historic contest. The temperatures hovered around minus 22 degrees Fahrenheit as the Oilers celebrated 25 years in the league. Led by Richard Zednik, the Canadiens beat the Oilers 4-3. Zednik got the Habs on the scoreboard with a second-period goal, and he got the game winner in the third.

13. GOT YOU COVERED

Game Plan:
Grasping God's protection

"For you ... who through faith are shielded by God's power."
1 PETER 1:4–5

Have you ever taken a good look at the gear covering an NHL goalie? The dude between the pipes looks like the Michelin Man with a mean facemask and a logo sewn on his sweater. You wonder how he can move with all that stuff on him.

NHL goalies are padded from head-to-toe—or so it seems. Former NHL netminder—and current NHL executive—Garth Snow was known for donning the biggest pads in the league. Then, a few years ago, the NHL began to cut down on the size of the pads that covered goaltenders. Snow and others were required to keep the width of their leg pads 12 inches or less. (With pucks traveling around 100 miles per hour, who can blame them for piling on the padding?)

FAST FACT:

The hardest slap shot ever recorded was by Chad Kilger during a skills competition in 2006. He fired a shot 106.6 miles per hour!

The walk of faith can be a lot like what an NHL goalie battling a power play endures. Day after day, we who are Christians face the speedy slap shots of life that can injure our faith. We battle shots of doubt, one-timers of discouragement, and rebounds of sinful temptation.

Like the NHL goalie, believers need protection. Just as the goalie needs his pads, gloves, helmet, and facemask, the follower of Christ needs a shield.

In his first letter, the apostle Peter teaches us that Christians do indeed have such protection.

Peter writes that through God, believers have "an inheritance that can never perish, spoil or fade—kept in heaven for you, who through faith are shielded by God's power until the coming of the salvation that is ready to be revealed in the last time"(1 Peter 1:4–5).

For those who have faith in Jesus, we are shielded by God's power! Now, there's something that can deflect the pucks of everyday life! And not merely in times of trouble. God promises to protect us in every situation until the day Jesus returns.

Christian, you are covered—even better than an NHL goalie.   —ROB BENTZ

FOLLOW THROUGH

Take a few moments to meditate on the significance of God's shielding love (v. 5) and His great salvation (vv. 5–9). Put these realities into your own words in a journal entry.

From the Playbook: Read 1 Peter 1:1–12.

THE LONGEST GAME March 24, 1936, Detroit Red Wings 1, Montreal Maroons 0—Imagine 176 minutes and 30 seconds of hockey—just three-and-a-half minutes short of three games—and just one goal. That's how long it took for the Detroit Red Wings and the Montreal Maroons to settle things in their showdown in the era between the two world wars. Wings' rookie Mud Bruneteau ended the game at 6:30 of the sixth overtime when he scored at 2:25 a.m. This was the first game of the first round of the playoffs, which Detroit went on to win.

14. IN THE MIDDLE OF A STRUGGLE

Game Plan:
Trusting God in the tough times

"In all things God works for the good of those who love him."
ROMANS 8:28

I am a competitive person. Every time I step on the ice, the goal for my team is to win.

I recall that one season with the Phoenix Coyotes we were off to a great start, winning our first three games—and that is just the way I like it. But before we knew it, we were struggling through an ugly winless streak.

Losing is no fun. Of course, for me to think that we can win all 82 games in an NHL season is simply unrealistic. I have had to learn a few things about how to handle a loss during my long career in the NHL.

FAST FACT:
Shane and Andrea Doan, who have four children, enjoy riding horses as a family.

One way to do that is that I choose to become more focused on winning the next game no matter what the outcome of the previous game, and to play with more intensity and determination. I try to encourage our players and bring out their strengths. I purpose to become a better teammate and player in spite of defeat.

In life, as in hockey, we can feel defeated by circumstances that come at us. In the midst of the struggle, it is hard to imagine that good can come out of difficult times. But God says it will. The Bible says that God causes everything to work for the good of those who love Him (Romans 8:28). He can take our times of defeat and work them out to give us something better.

I realize that sometimes our team may not finish as high in the standings as I would want—despite how hard we will play. But I can still trust that God has a purpose for me in this—just as He has for every detail of my life, because I love Him and am "called according to his purpose" (v. 28).

Are you in the middle of a struggle—a loss? Keep trusting God.
—SHANE DOAN

FOLLOW THROUGH

Is there a situation in your life today that seems to be defeating you? Is there anything you can do to change the situation? When the situation is out of your hands, what can you do place it in God's hands?

From the Playbook: Read James 1:2–8.

TOP 25 GREAT HOCKEY GAMES

PETR "THE BABE" SYKORA   June 2, 2008, Pittsburgh Penguins 4, Detroit Red Wings 3—It's not often that a hockey player is somehow equated to a baseball player, but this time it works. Sort of. The Pittsburgh Penguins were taking on the Detroit Red Wings in Game 5 of the Stanley Cup Finals. The two teams were deadlocked at 3-3 as they headed into overtime. That's when Sykora told a network TV broadcaster that he would win the game with a goal—perhaps a little like Babe Ruth's called home run in the 1932 World Series. Three overtimes into the contest, at 9:57, Sykora did as he said he would—he scored to give the Penguins the win.

15. "DEAR DOMINIC"

"Salvation is found in no one else, for there is no other name under heaven given to men by which we must be saved." ACTS 4:12

When former National Hockey League goalie Dominic Roussel was still just a junior hockey star, he received "The Invitation."

It wasn't a formal calligraphy-and-parchment-paper type invitation to the most prestigious social event in town. This invitation, sent from then-NHL star Ryan Walter, was just a normal piece of paper written from one hockey player to another.

The letter Roussel received was an invitation to attend a Billy Graham Crusade where Walter was scheduled to speak. Roussel was interested immediately. He had been reading his Bible and searching for the way to heaven, but he had yet to find it. So Roussel accepted the invitation.

At the crusade, the young goalie listened intently as Walter detailed how putting his faith in Jesus Christ had changed his life and the lives of other players in the NHL. Walter told of the eternal life he now possessed because of forgiveness offered by Christ.

Roussel had found the way to heaven!

That night, Dominic Roussel made an invitation of his own: he asked Jesus Christ to forgive his sins and be his Savior.

He joined a growing list of NHL players who play a physically demanding game that includes lots of rough play and a

FAST FACT:
Ryan Walter's three sons all have played at the college level and above in hockey. His son Ben has played for several NHL teams.

bit of controlled mayhem but who also have put their faith in Jesus Christ. Men such as Shane Doan, Mike Gartner, Cam Ward, Jarome Iginla, and Mike Fisher.

If you too are looking for the way to heaven, the Bible teaches us that Jesus is the only way. Have you invited Jesus into your life? Receive eternal life today by talking with God. Say something like this:

God, I confess that I am a sinner. I accept the forgiveness that your Son Jesus offers me because of what He did on the cross. Beginning today, I want to live for you. I want to spend eternity with you in heaven. I invite Jesus Christ to be the Lord of my life. Thank you for saving me. Amen!   —ROB BENTZ

FOLLOW THROUGH

Have you answered Jesus' invitation to you? If so, have you invited anyone else to meet Jesus?

From the Playbook: Read John 3:1–16.

TOP 25 GREAT HOCKEY GAMES

THE COLD WAR **October 6, 2001, Michigan 3, Michigan State 3**—The two big boys of Michigan college sports started a revolution in 2001. It was called the Cold War, and it pitted the University of Michigan against Michigan State University in an outdoor hockey game. The Spartans constructed a rink at Spartan Stadium for the game, and 74,544 fans showed up. It was the biggest crowd ever to see one hockey game. Although the teams didn't settle anything on the ice—the game ended in a 3-3 tie, this game set the stage for other outdoor hockey games worldwide.

16. THINK FAST!

"My grace is sufficient for you." 2 CORINTHIANS 12:9

Eighteen thousand screaming fans surround you. You are protecting a tiny sliver of ice in front of a net. Suddenly, a puck comes off the stick of an opposing player, and it is angling toward your head.

What would you do?

a. Duck.
b. Snare it for an outstanding save.
c. Wake up from your dream and admit that you're really not a pro hockey goalie.

Did you pick "a"? That's okay. I feel the same way about objects hurtling at me in excess of 100 mph. However, "c" is probably the right answer for most of us.

FAST FACT:

If a hockey player were to take a shot from the blue line, and if the puck were to be going 90 mph, the goalie would have four-tenths of a second to react before it reaches the crease.

I mean, you have to be one tough humanoid to tend the net in professional hockey. Take Larry Dyck, for example. He played in the International Hockey League for several seasons in the 1980s and 1990s.

He was a good goalie. He was tough. He was determined. And he had been legally blind in one eye since childhood.

How did Larry handle those laser-like shots at the net? "In hockey, the puck comes so fast you don't have to worry about perception," he explains.

Pretty humble response, huh? In reality, this gutsy goalie played well in a position that requires lightning-quick reflexes, incredible coordination, and superb vision.

The apostle Paul was another man who did a job well even though he had a serious challenge. Paul's disability was a "thorn in the flesh" (2 Corinthians 12:7). While we don't know what his affliction was, we can be sure that it was bothersome and painful. He pleaded with God three times to take it away, but He let it stay.

Why? Paul heard this reply from God: "My grace is sufficient for you, for my power is made perfect in weakness" (2 Corinthians 12:9).

Sometimes the things we wrestle with—physical impairments, emotional challenges, sickness—bring us to the place God wants us to be: broken and ready to do His work in His power alone. I know. I've battled cancer.

So, keep your eyes open—and be ready at any time to stop some pucks.

—TOM FELTEN

FOLLOW THROUGH

What challenge do you feel you need to overcome? Is there anyone else you know about with the same problem? Why not talk to him or her about it?

From the Playbook: Read 2 Corinthians 12:7–10.

GREAT HOCKEY GAMES

SUPERSTAR VS. SUPERSTAR **May 4, 2009, Washington Capitals 4, Pittsburgh Penguins 3**—This is exactly what you want to see happen when two mega-stars go head to head. It's like Sandy Koufax pitching against Bob Gibson. Or LeBron James' team taking on Kobe Bryant's. Or Phil Mickelson battling Tiger Woods on Sunday. This time: Sidney Crosby vs. Alex Ovechkin. Pittsburgh vs. Washington. Game 2, Eastern Conference finals. Both players cost a lot of fans a lot of hats as they each recorded hat tricks. By the way, the Caps won 4-3.

17. TOO YOUNG?

Game Plan:
Making an impact for God

*"Don't let anyone look down on you because you are
young, but set an example for the believers."*

1 TIMOTHY 4:12

When he was only 18 years old, Sidney Crosby became the
first pick in the 2005 National Hockey League Draft.

All he did after being drafted was to go out and finish sixth
in the league in points while helping to revitalize the Pittsburgh Penguins. A year later, Crosby followed up his phenom-
enal rookie year by leading the NHL in scoring, winning the
league's Most Valuable Player Award, along with
two other prestigious awards.

All before he was 20—pretty amazing stuff,
huh?

And while being compared to one of the
greatest players of all time, Wayne Gretzky,
Crosby—known as Sid the Kid—never let his
youthfulness get in the way of making an
impact. In fact, he was only 22 when he marked
his name forever in the annals of Canadian
hockey history by scoring the overtime goal to
give Canada the gold medal in the 2010 Olympic Winter Games over the US in Vancouver.

FAST FACT:
*In the 2006–07
NHL season, Sid-
ney Crosby
became the first
teen in any North
American pro
sports league to
lead his sport in
scoring (120
points).*

Have you ever thought about doing something for God?
Have you ever stopped yourself from doing it because you
thought you were too young or not important enough? That's
not what Jesus wants you to think. In 1 Timothy 4, young
Timothy is called to be used by God despite his young age.

Instructed not to let anyone look down on his youthfulness, he is called to be an example for other Christians (v. 12).

God is bigger than anyone you may encounter, so if He's given you the ability to do something big, don't let others who may say you're not old enough get in the way of that. Daniel and David are biblical examples of how God can use young people for His glory. Be like them.

God has blessed us all—regardless of our age and life's experience—with special gifts, and He expects us to make an impact on His kingdom by putting those gifts to good use.

—JEFF ARNOLD

FOLLOW THROUGH

Take some time to think about the gifts God has given you. Are you using them to their full extent, or are you making excuses why you shouldn't be used by God? If you are, ask God to help you make the most of your skills to reach others for Jesus.

From the Playbook: Read 1 Timothy 4.

TOP 25 GREAT HOCKEY GAMES

HIGH OCTANE OILERS! **December 11, 1985, Edmonton Oilers 12, Chicago Blackhawks 9**—The Edmonton Oilers and the Chicago Blackhawks put the most points on the board of any two teams in modern NHL history when the Oilers beat the Hawks 12-9. While the Oilers' Wayne Gretzky didn't score, he had seven assists. Jari Kurri and Glenn Anderson both recorded hat tricks. There were 11 goals scored in the second period alone. The score was 10-6 after the second period.

18. TURNED AWAY

*"No one can see the kingdom of God
unless he is born again."* JOHN 3:3

Have you ever tried doing something for someone, only to have it backfire? I have.

A few years ago, I decided to take my father-in-law to a Buffalo Sabres home hockey game. The last-place Sabres were scheduled to battle the next-to-last-place Tampa Bay Lightning during a down year for both teams. I had kept my eye on Sabres' attendance figures for a few days and noticed they had not been selling out the HSBC Arena. So I assumed that walk-up tickets would be no problem. (Can you see where this is going?)

FAST FACT:

The HSBC Arena in Buffalo, which was built in 1996, seats 18,690 people for hockey. There is also an HSBC Arena in Rio de Janeiro, Brazil. HSBC is a banking group.

As we walked up to the ticket window, the lady behind the plexiglas smiled warmly. I asked for the two best seats available. She smiled again, then gave us the bad news. "We have just singles left."

"What?" I said in disbelief. "Only single seats for a Sabres-Lightning game? You don't have two seats together anywhere in the building?"

"Nope," she replied, somehow still smiling.

I wasn't getting two seats together, and I wasn't smiling.

A night of hard-checking hockey action was cast aside faster than a Martin Biron kick-save. Why? Because I had not prepared properly. How embarrassing!

While my lack of planning left me a bit ashamed and unable to impress my father-in-law, something a whole lot more ugly could happen to you and to me if we are not prepared for an event far more important than any NHL game. I'm talking about eternity. The Bible teaches us that in order to spend eternity with God in heaven, we must be born again.

Have you placed your eternal life in the hands of Jesus Christ? Don't be turned away. Reserve your spot in heaven by putting your faith in Jesus Christ today.   —ROB BENTZ

FOLLOW THROUGH

Seriously, are you ready to meet God? It may be possible to live in this world without acknowledging Him or feeling you have to deal with Him, but eventually you have to account to Him for your sins. Only faith in Christ can give you hope of eternal joy.

From the Playbook: Read Romans 5:12–21.

TOP 25 GREAT HOCKEY GAMES

CZECH MATE   **February 20, 1998**—Dominik Hasek may have been an NHL mate for the Canadians who were playing in the 1998 Winter Olympics, but he was definitely their nemesis as the Czech Republic and Canada tangled in the semifinals. The Dominator's 24 saves helped the Czechs go into overtime tied at 1-1. Then Hasek turned back all of Canada's shots in a shootout, enabling Robert Reichel's goal to be the game-winner and send the Czechs against Russia in the finals. Hasek shut out the Russians 1-0, and the CR took home gold from Nagano.

19. CAPTAIN COYOTE

Game Plan:
Practicing encouragement

*"Speaking the truth in love, we will in all
things grow up into him who is the Head,
that is, Christ."* EPHESIANS 4:15

I still recall how grateful and humbled I was to be selected as
the captain of the Phoenix Coyotes for the first time back
in 2003. To serve my teammates in this way was both a great
honor and a great responsibility.

When it comes to team motivation, there was a range of
styles I could have chosen to try to help the Coyotes. I could
jump on every little mistake my teammates
made and tear guys apart in front of the team,
or I could pat everyone on the back and say,
"Good job," regardless of how well or how
poorly they might play. But neither approach
would help a team be the best. The first one
chips away at the players' confidence; the second excuses away any need for improvement.

I found it difficult at first to be more vocal
with the players about their game. By nature
I am an encourager. I'd love to be able to just
highlight the positives and tell everyone they
were doing great. But if I was going to do the
best for my team, sometimes that required talking with a
player about areas where he was struggling and challenging
him to improve.

In Ephesians 4:15–16, Paul writes about the need for us
to grow up as believers and grow together as one body in
Christ, each depending on the other. This is a great model for

team building. As believers, we will never grow into a complete body unless we are willing to speak God's truth to one another—not to find fault and tear down in judgment, but to counsel and encourage in humility and love.

Who are the people who have most encouraged your growth in the Lord? What was it they said or did that was most effective? Is there someone in your circle of believers who needs both encouragement and advice from you?

—SHANE DOAN

FOLLOW THROUGH

Are there some people you need to send an e-mail to today, just to let them know you think they are pretty important? Make a note of it, and be an encourager.

From the Playbook: Read 1 Thessalonians 5:11–15.

GREAT HOCKEY GAMES

KINGED! **April 10, 1982, LA Kings 6, Edmonton Oilers 5**—This appeared to be no contest. It was the Smythe Division semifinals, and the Edmonton Oilers seemed invincible. During the regular season, they had accumulated nearly twice the standings points that their opponents, the LA Kings, had mustered. So when Wayne Gretzky and the Oilers jumped out to a 5-0 lead after two periods, the party appeared to be over for LA. But the Kings didn't get the memo. The Kings battled back and tied the game with five seconds left. Then Daryl Evans won it in overtime for LA, who went on to eliminate the Oilers.

20. REMARKABLE FORGIVENESS

"Be kind and compassionate to one another, forgiving each other, just as in Christ God forgave you." EPHESIANS 4:32

Dany Heatley could have gone to prison. Instead, he went to the Olympics.

Dan Snyder's family could have gone for the jugular. Instead, they went for forgiveness.

The names of Dany Heatley and Dan Snyder will forever be etched together in NHL history. In September 2003, Heatley and Snyder were teammates and friends on the Atlanta Thrashers.

One day they got into Dany Heatley's Ferrari for an early fall drive. Both were seriously injured when the Ferrari flew off the road and crashed. Heatley survived. Snyder—the innocent party—did not. Head injuries claimed his life.

Graham Snyder and his family could have thrown the book at the man who killed their son. Their dreams shattered, they could have shattered Dany's life too.

But something stopped Snyder and his family from doing that. Something called faith. Something they learned as a strong Christian family.

Although he could have asked a judge to go after Heatley on a charge of vehicular homicide, Graham Snyder didn't. Instead, he asked the judge not to send Heatley to jail. He didn't—sentencing Heatley to serve three years' probation.

FAST FACT:

Dan Snyder's parents have formed the Dan Snyder Foundation to provide scholarships, and they helped raise money for the Dan Snyder Memorial Arena in Elmira, Ontario, Canada. The need for this arena was something Dan and his dad talked about just weeks before he died in 2003.

The Snyders knew something important about forgiveness. It lets life go on. Blaming, accusing, finger pointing—those all stop life in its tracks and bury people under the rubble of pain. Forgiveness, Graham Snyder said, helped his family "move on."

"We are all human beings, and we know that humans make mistakes," Snyder said. "We do not lay blame on Dany Heatley for the accident that took our son from us ..." There is nothing to gain from harboring resentment or anger toward others.

They knew the story of Peter and Jesus.

When Peter asked Jesus how many times he should forgive someone, the Rock figured he could cover forgiveness by doing it seven times. But Jesus surprised Peter by telling him it took 77 times to forgive (Matthew 18:22).

Jesus' words seem to suggest the concept of never-ending forgiveness. How much better it is for us to forgive more times than we have to instead of holding back.

It's one more way of looking up to the Father and thanking Him for the forgiveness He lavished on us.   —DAVE BRANON

FOLLOW THROUGH

Who do you need to forgive? Is there someone whose life would suddenly be a lot better if you would simply say, "I forgive you"?

From the Playbook: Read Matthew 18:21–35.

GREAT HOCKEY GAMES

MEHRARBEIT LEISTEN   March 22, 2008, Cologne Sharks 5, Mannheim Eagles 4—It means, "To work overtime," which is what the Cologne Sharks and the Mannheim Eagles did in the longest German hockey game ever. The game went six overtimes (108 overtime minutes) before Philip Gogulla of the Sharks gave them a 5-4 win over the Eagles. The game took nearly seven hours to play.

21. WE'RE ALL GOALIES

Game Plan:
Grasping God's gifting

"If [we] were all one part, where would the body be?
As it is, there are many parts, but one body."
1 CORINTHIANS 12:19–20

Playing goalie is weird. There's no other way to look at it. Consider the facts: Your positioning on the ice is opposite every other player. You never have a chance to score. Even the gear is different. Truth is, it takes an entirely different skill set to play between the pipes.

FAST FACT:

Between 2000 and 2010, only two goalies were inducted into the Hockey Hall of Fame—Grant Fuhr and Patrick Roy.

Skills like shuffling, telescoping, sweeping, and butterfly are critical to the goalie's success. Yet none of these skills are required for any other player on the ice. The goaltender is an odd one!

Regarding our role in God's kingdom, we're all goaltenders. We all have talents, gifts, and abilities that are different from other Christ-followers. God made us that way for a purpose.

In his first letter to the church in Corinth, the apostle Paul writes of the importance of the diversity of our God-given gifts within the church—the Body of Christ. "But in fact God has arranged the parts in the body, every one of them, just as he wanted them to be. If they were all one part, where would the body be?" (1 Corinthians 12:18–19).

If everyone happened to be a defenseman, where would the scoring be? If everyone played center, how would we keep the puck inside the blue line? In hockey, as in life, we all play a key part in a much bigger picture.

54

The skills that make a goaltender so important to a hockey team give us a great picture of the individual skills that set you apart from others and make you vital to God's grand plan. The uniqueness of who you are is just the way God made you. He wanted you to be different because He can—and will—use your difference and uniqueness to build and serve His kingdom.

Rejoice in that fact that like a goalie—you are different. Celebrate your unique gifts and put them to work for God and His kingdom.

—ROB BENTZ

FOLLOW THROUGH

Read through the list of spiritual gifts listed in 1 Corinthians 12:8–11 and the others listed in verses 28–31. Ask God to reveal how He has gifted you, and ask Him to give you understanding of how you can best use your gift(s).

From the Playbook: Read 1 Corinthians 12:12–31.

TOP 25 GREAT HOCKEY GAMES

TERRIERS ATTACK REDHAWKS **April 12, 2009, Boston University 4, Miami University 3**—In the 2009 NCAA national championship game between the Miami University RedHawks and the Boston University Terriers, BU put together what some say is the most dramatic hockey comeback ever. With the national title on the line, Miami entered the final minute of play with a 3-1 lead. The students back in Oxford, Ohio, were 60 seconds away from a campus-wide party. But Nick Bonino became Mr. Party Pooper. First, his pass led to one Boston goal, and then with 17 ticks left, he scored the tying goal. The Terriers then scored in OT, and the party shifted to Beantown.

22. CREATE A MONUMENT

Game Plan:
Remembering the fallen

"Do this in remembrance of me."
1 CORINTHIANS 11:24

When Brett Hull skated onto the ice during the 2004 pre-season for a Red Wings inter-squad game, he wasn't wearing his familiar No. 17. Instead, he was wearing No. 80 in honor of Herb Brooks.

Brooks, who is most famous for coaching the 1980 US Olympic hockey team to its "Miracle on Ice" gold medal, died in a car accident in August 2003. Hull, who had spoken with Brooks the night before his untimely death, said about wearing the former coach's number: "It's just kind of to honor a great man and a great coach, just to keep him on people's minds."

FAST FACT:
Herb Brooks played for the US Olympic team in both 1964 and 1968.

Hull was doing what so many people who have lost a loved one do—create monuments that will help ensure that the person's memory lives on.

One of the fears that took me by surprise when I lost a close family member several years ago was that this deceased person would eventually drift from our minds. I feared that people (including myself) would forget the special and kind-hearted person she was. I've sensed the same concern as I've witnessed friends and co-workers lose a child, a husband, a dad, a brother.

Remembering those who meant so much to us is critical as we move forward with our new life without them. They are forever linked to our story and will always be a part of who we are. To forget what they meant to us is to forget a part of who we are.

I believe this is one reason Jesus, within hours of His death and resurrection, instructed His disciples and all who followed Him to make it a habit to remember Him (1 Corinthians 11:23–25). Remembering our Lord's life, death, and resurrection isn't only a part of us—it's the very heart of who we are.

Whatever it takes, never forget those who have gone on before. —JEFF OLSON

FOLLOW THROUGH

If you don't already, make time to remember and reflect on the life, death, and resurrection of Jesus Christ.

From the Playbook: Read 1 Corinthians 15:3–4.

TOP 25 — GREAT HOCKEY GAMES

MIRACULOUS **February 22, 1980, United States 4, Russia 3**—
Not much was expected from the US team on February 22, 1980. After all, the US squad consisted of college kids and other amateurs, and their Russian opponents in the Olympic Winter Games in Lake Placid, New York, were pros who had beaten NHL teams. Indeed, a fortnight earlier, the Soviets had manhandled the young Yanks 10-3. But you do believe in miracles, don't you? Miracles like a kid from Massachusetts named Mike Eruzione scoring the game-winning goal for the red, white, and blue—and then the US holding on to get to the finals of the Olympics. *Sports Illustrated* called the 1980 "Do you believe in Miracles?" game the "Greatest Sports Moment of the Century."

23. ZACH AND THE KID

"Blessed is the man who perseveres under trial."

JAMES 1:12

With 24.4 seconds left in one of the biggest hockey games of all-time, Zach Parise broke through the defense of the Canadian national team and scored a goal that sent Americans into a short season of joy.

Parise was, momentarily, a hero in the United States. His goal put the American team into overtime with Team Canada for the gold medal in the 2010 Olympic Winter Games in Vancouver. Because of Parise's goal, the Yankees could take home the coveted medal with one single goal. After trailing 2-0 for much of the game, they could still win.

FAST FACT:

Both Zach Parise and Sidney Crosby were alternate captains for their respective teams in the 2010 Olympic Winter Games.

However, things didn't turn out that way. As it happened, Parise's goal gave a Canadian player, namely Sidney Crosby, the chance to be the hero. When he swooped in on the left side of the goal, swept up a pass from Jarome Iginla, and fired it past Ryan Miller for the win, it was Canada's turn to rejoice. Sid the Kid, not Zach Parise, became the national hero.

Amazing, isn't it, how things change? Instead of Parise's goal cementing his name in Olympic history as a hero, it instead opened the door for Crosby to climb up next to Paul Henderson in the annals of Canadian hockey history. It would have been easy for Crosby and his teammates to have caved in after Parise's goal—to let that goal deplete them and then fail to score in overtime.

What a mirror to life! Encouraging triumphs can sometimes lead to surprising sadness. Down times can turn into seasons of joy. In James 1, the writer says that sometimes going through tough times is what leads to the joy Christ has in store for a person. That's why the key to moving through life is to not let our daily circumstances control our attitude and our goals. Instead, "persevere under trial"(4:12) and trust God for the outcome. —DAVE BRANON

FOLLOW THROUGH

Is there a situation right now in your life that isn't looking good? How do you think God wants you to treat that situation so it can eventually turn out better?

From the Playbook: Read James 1:1–15.

TOP 25
GREAT HOCKEY GAMES

THE KID WINS IT **February 28, 2010, Canada 3, United States 2**—It was easy for American hockey fans to forget that Sidney "The Kid" Crosby was Canadian. After all, what's more American than Pittsburgh—where Crosby skated for the Penguins? But in the gold medal game of the 2010 Olympic Winter Games, Crosby reminded everyone that he's a Maple Leaf at heart. Seven minutes and forty seconds into overtime as the US and Canada battled for Olympics supremacy, Crosby took a pass from Jarome Iginla and scooted the puck under Ryan Miller's pads to light the lamp and make the Canadians the first home-ice gold medal winners in the Olympics since the Americans did it at Lake Placid in 1980.

24. THE APPRENTICE

"Be diligent in these matters."
1 TIMOTHY 4:15

On May 25, 2010, longtime Detroit Red Wings superstar Steve Yzerman left the only NHL organization he had ever known. On that day, much to the shock of Red Wings fans, Yzerman was named the new general manager of the Tampa Bay Lightning.

After amassing a Hall of Fame career that included 692 goals, 1,755 points, and three Stanley Cups as a player, Yzerman had moved into the Detroit front office as a team vice-president. In spite of the fancy title, Yzerman went to work as an apprentice to Detroit general manager Ken Holland learning the finer details (i.e. managing rosters, working under a salary cap, negotiations, etc.) of running an NHL club. Both Yzerman and the Red Wings enjoyed even more success—winning a fourth Stanley Cup in 2008.

FAST FACT:

Steve Yzerman was inducted into the Hockey Hall of Fame in 2009. Joining him in the Class of 2009 were former Red Wing teammates Brett Hull and Luc Robitaille, along with Brian Leetch and Lou Lamoriello.

Yzerman was a gifted athlete with a deep passion to succeed. The same passion that made him a Hall of Fame player helped him in his work of rebuilding the Tampa Bay Lightning as he used the front-office skills he learned from his mentors.

The Word of God contains many stories of men and women who worked diligently to fulfill God's calling on their lives. The apostle Paul's understudy Timothy was one such man.

Initially, Timothy was a timid young man who lacked confidence (1 Timothy 4:12). Yet God had clearly given him the ability to lead the church (v. 13). Timothy had grown and progressed under Paul's tutelage (v. 15) and was counseled by his mentor to lead the church in integrity of life and doctrine (v. 16).

The words Paul wrote to Timothy can serve as a guide for you and me as well. As you move into a role of added responsibility—trust in your God-given gifts, recall what you've been taught, be diligent to grow, and live with integrity as you stand firm on the historical doctrines of the faith.   —ROB BENTZ

FOLLOW THROUGH

Ask God, through prayer, if there is someone you should be learning from through a mentoring or apprenticeship role. If so, take the next step and ask that individual to mentor you.

From the Playbook: Read 1 Timothy 4:12–16.

TOP 25 GREAT HOCKEY GAMES

GOING FOR BORQUE   June 9, 2001, Colorado Avalanche 3, New Jersey Devils 1—After 22 seasons. After 1,826 NHL games. After a couple of nations got on the Ray Borque bandwagon, the Colorado Avalanche beat the New Jersey Devils 3-1 in Game 7 of the 2001 Stanley Cup Finals to give the Quebec native his first NHL championship. And then he retired. He had waited longer than any other player in NHL history to win his first Stanley Cup.

25. KEEP AN EYE ON HIM!

Game Plan:
Making sure your life is worth watching

"Say 'No' to ungodliness and worldly passions, and . . . live self-controlled, upright and godly lives." TITUS 2:12

You would think a bunch of hard-driving hockey players wouldn't have a moment of fear for someone as non-threatening as a Christian.

But that wasn't the case with the National Hockey League team the Washington Capitals many years ago when they acquired right-winger Jean Pronovost from the Atlanta Flames (before that franchise pulled up stakes and headed to Calgary).

FAST FACT:
Pronovost played in nearly 1,000 NHL games between 1968 and 1982. During the 1975–76 season, he scored 104 points for the Pittsburgh Penguins.

As soon as Pronovost joined the team, the players were warned: "Keep an eye on the new guy." He was a Christian, and apparently to some folks in hockey, that means he's dangerous.

Two teammates who watched Pronovost closely were up-and-coming NHL stars Mike Gartner (who had recently moved over from the World Hockey Association) and Ryan Walter (who was in his third year in the league). As Mike and Ryan observed his life, they didn't see anything to be afraid of. In fact, they both saw something they liked—his Christian testimony.

Soon Mike and Ryan were attending Bible studies with Jean. And in time both players trusted Jesus Christ as Savior through Pronovost's influence. Still today, though retired from the NHL, Gartner and Walter continue to maintain a strong witness about their faith.

What is it about genuine Christians that some people find irresistible? The apostle Paul talked about those inviting qualities in his letter to Titus. He mentioned traits such as self-control (2:6), good works, integrity, seriousness (v. 7), and a life about which no one can speak evil (v. 8).

If you are a Christian, does that describe you? Just as they were with Pronovost, others are keeping an eye on you. They want to know if there's anything genuine about this idea of being a follower of Jesus.

Heed Paul's advice and make sure your life is worth watching.

—DAVE BRANON

FOLLOW THROUGH

What are three characteristics you have that might attract others to Christ? Are there any negative characteristics that you might want to eliminate?

From the Playbook: Read Titus 2.

TOP 25 GREAT HOCKEY GAMES

THE UNLIKELY AMERICAN   April 23, 1950, Detroit Red Wings 4, New York Rangers 3—Back in the day, it was unusual for an American player to earn his living in the NHL. The Detroit Red Wings had one, however, in 1950: Braeburn, Pennsylvania's Pete Babando. In Game 7 of the Stanley Cup finals, Babando scored in double overtime to give the Wings a 4-3 win over the New York Rangers, and he became an unlikely hero in his own country.

26. SEEK WISDOM AND UNDERSTANDING

Game Plan:
Living by God's standards

"The fear of the Lord is the beginning of wisdom."
PSALM 111:10

Decades after his successful tenure at UCLA, John Wooden remains one of the most respected basketball coaches in history. The UCLA Bruins' athletic teams have recorded the most NCAA sports championships of all time (more than 100), and nearly 10 percent of their titles were won by one man: Wooden. As the coach of the UCLA basketball team in the 1960s and 1970s, Wooden won 10 NCAA titles.

Born in 1910, Coach Wooden was still publishing books about coaching, life, and faith at the age of 99. He died in June 2010, a little more than four months short of his 100th birthday. And his legacy endures.

Columnist Rick Reilly wrote of the coach before he died, "Of the 180 players who played for him, [he] knows the whereabouts of 172. Of course, it's not hard when most of them call, checking on his health, secretly hoping to hear some of his simple life lessons that they can write on the lunch bags of their kids... Never lie, never cheat, never steal. Earn the right to be proud and confident."

His legacy reflects a life-long pursuit of a creed his father gave him when he was 12 years old and formed the basis of Wooden's influence through the years.

FAST FACT:

In Coach Wooden's last nine years at the helm at UCLA, the Bruins lost a total of 12 games (259-12).

1. Be true to yourself. 2. Help others. 3. Make each day your masterpiece. 4. Drink deeply from good books, especially the Bible. 5. Make friendship a fine art. 6. Build a shelter against a rainy day. 7. Pray for guidance and give thanks for your blessings every day.

Coach Wooden did his best to live by this creed, and as a result his life was a masterpiece that enriched the lives of people everywhere.

Consider living by principles such as those above, which can help you follow Proverbs 2:2. It suggests "turning your ear to wisdom and applying your heart to understanding."

—ROXANNE ROBBINS

FOLLOW THROUGH

Write down Wooden's principles on a piece of paper. Put them in your pocket and take them with you—thinking about what they say throughout the day.

From the Playbook: Read Proverbs 1:1–6.

GREAT BASKETBALL GAMES

HOOPS GOES BIG-TIME   January 20, 1968, Houston 71, UCLA 69—Imagine this. Before Elvin Hayes went up against Lew Alcindor at the Houston Astrodome on this date, there had never been a nationally televised, regular season college basketball game. The draw for this one? Two undefeated teams with the two best men in college hoops going head to head. The UCLA Bruins were No. 1 and Hayes' Houston Cougars were ranked No. 2. But the Cougars won 71-69 in front of 52,693 folks in the house and millions around the country, and they remained No. 1 until losing to UCLA in the national semifinals.

27. NOT-SO-FUNDAMENTAL

Game Plan:
Going over the basics

"I give you this instruction." 1 TIMOTHY 1:18

In 1992 the Chicago Bulls were in the heyday of their first dynasty. The NBA Finals put the Portland Trail Blazers on the platter for the Bulls to devour. This series was billed by the media as Clyde "the Glide" Drexler versus Michael "Air" Jordan. Also grabbing headlines were writers who questioned the Trail Blazers' basketball knowledge because they played with emotion and athleticism but appeared to have no use for the fundamentals. Perhaps that is the reason they blew a lead in Game 6 after leading by 15 points—and maybe that's why the Blazers lost the series.

FAST FACT:
Michael Jordan hit six 3-pointers and scored 35 points in the first half of Game 1 of the 1992 NBA Finals—both new records.

Fundamentals are essential—in basketball, in life, and most notably in our efforts to grow as Christians. Paul told Timothy this in the first book by the same name. Timothy, dude, don't disregard the basic instruction I've given. Paul warned that if he did, he would risk what he called spiritual shipwreck. For us to refuse to use spiritual instruction to fight the good fight would be dumb—dumb because we've got the God-given skills. But we won't win this spiritual fight with just our emotion and skill. We need the fundamentals.

I was in Chicago in 1992, and I watched the Trail Blazers practice a few times. One day, after the media left the building, the coach got the team together and preached the fundamentals. The full-court scrimmage that followed was quite a spectacle. The speed, grace, and athleticism that roared up and down the court was like a freight train. That night, the basic instruction combined with their skills won the game for them. But later in the series, they got away from the fundamentals and lost.

Don't you lose the series; your life may depend on it. Practice the fundamentals of the faith. —Dan Deal

FOLLOW THROUGH

What godly fundamentals do you know but aren't using? To shipwreck is serious, so stick with the instruction found in the Scriptures.

From the Playbook: Read 1 Timothy 1:12–18.

TOP 25 GREAT BASKETBALL GAMES

A TASTE OF THINGS TO COME **March 30, 1982, North Carolina 63, Georgetown 62**—The lineups were sprinkled with names that were destined for NBA stardom. James Worthy. Sam Perkins. Patrick Ewing. But the one who rose above all others on this night—and the one who would eventually be known as the best player in the game—was Michael Jordan. With 15 seconds left, Jordan hit a 16-foot jump shot that gave the North Carolina Tar Heels a 63-62 win over the Georgetown Hoyas in the national championship game. That shot began to propel him into the stratosphere of basketball stardom.

28. THE SHOT THAT MADE MARCH MAD

Game Plan:
Knowing our spiritual foe

"The accuser of our brothers ... has been hurled down."
REVELATION 12:10

Aside from the championships my alma mater (Michigan State) has claimed, my favorite March Madness memory is Lorenzo Charles' dunk off a desperation air ball in 1983. His put-back gave North Carolina State an improbable 54-52 victory over the mighty Houston Cougars. *Sporting News* called it "the shot that made March mad."

Houston, with superstar players such as Hakeem Olajuwon and Clyde Drexler, had won 26 consecutive games, most of them in dominating fashion. North Carolina State had 10 losses, and the Wolfpack had barely gotten past Pepperdine in the tournament! Except for Houston alums—and perhaps North Carolina Tar Heel fans—the game was a fitting conclusion to the tournament that helped birth the phrase "March Madness."

FAST FACT:

In 1983, North Carolina State won seven of its last nine games after trailing in the final minute.

Jim Valvano and North Carolina State faced a formidable foe and won.

We should know about foes. But we all face a far more ominous adversary than Phi Slamma Jamma (Houston's colorful nickname). It's the enemy of our souls, Satan the accuser (Revelation 12:10). He hates us, and no amount of willpower will enable us to defeat him.

Thankfully, we have a prayer—and a champion. He's Jesus Christ, who has conquered both sin and death. Paul wrote that the penalty for sin is death, "but the gift of God is eternal life in Christ Jesus our Lord" (Romans 6:23). He also told us, "The sting of death is sin ... but thanks be to God! He gives us victory through our Lord Jesus Christ" (1 Corinthians 15:56).

Without Jesus, we are at the mercy of our adversary. But when we are in Him, our "labor in the Lord is not in vain" (1 Corinthians 15:58). The last enemy has been defeated. We win!   —TIM GUSTAFSON

FOLLOW THROUGH

Do I face my difficulties and challenges alone, in my own strength? What does my answer reveal about my own pride? Why is it foolish to reject Jesus' offer of salvation—and ultimate victory?

From the Playbook: Read 1 Corinthians 15:50–58.

GREAT BASKETBALL GAMES

JIMMY V'S MOMENT   April 4, 1983, North Carolina State 54, Houston 52—You cannot think of shining moments in NCAA college hoops history without thinking of North Carolina State's coach Jimmy Valvano's celebratory dash across the floor of The Pit in Albuquerque, New Mexico. When Dereck Whittenburg's desperation air ball found Lorenzo Charles' waiting hands, and he turned Dereck's disaster into the Wolfpack's wonder—it appeared that anything could happen. NC State didn't seem to have a chance against the high-flying Cougars of Houston: Hakeem Olajuwon, Clyde Drexler, et al. But miracles happen, and Wolfpacks fly! College basketball would never be the same because Jimmy V and his guys beat Houston 54-52.

29. PISTOL PETE'S SEARCH

Game Plan:
Looking and finding God's peace

"What good will it be for a man if he gains the whole world, yet forfeits his soul?" MATTHEW 16:26

Pistol Pete Maravich is considered one of basketball's all-time great players. While at LSU, Maravich averaged 44.2 points per game—the highest average in NCAA history. He starred professionally as well, drawing record audiences during his NBA career with the Atlanta Hawks, New Orleans Jazz, and Boston Celtics. Julius Erving says Maravich was a "basketball genius." The NBA agreed and selected Maravich as one of the top 50 players in NBA history in 1996 when the league celebrated 50 years of operation.

Maravich earned basketball stardom, but in his autobiography he explained that there was a time he wanted to die because of mistakes he committed in other parts of his life.

On December 31, 1977, Maravich wrote in his journal: "I pray that before I'm through with this entire life of mine, I will be happy, peaceful, and my mind at ease about life and God. How can I be unhappy? It is very simple. There are millions of people who have not found a deep sense of purpose and meaning. I am one of them... With all the trophies, awards, money, and fame; I am not at peace with myself."

When he was little, Pete's dad challenged him that if he put his total energy into basketball, he could be a star—and he could be rich. It happened just as Press Maravich said. However, happiness didn't come with that glory and fame and wealth.

Five years after Maravich penned the above words, though, he found the peace he desperately craved—peace that came when he cried out to God pleading for forgiveness, saying, "Jesus, I know you're real because I've tried everything else. I've got nowhere to go. If you don't save me, I won't last two more days."

Maravich wrote that it was at that moment his life changed forever: "When I took God into my heart, it was the first true happiness I ever had."

The Lord gave Maravich peace. Have you asked Him to do the same for you?

—ROXANNE ROBBINS

FOLLOW THROUGH

Pistol Pete wanted to be remembered as a person who served Christ. What do you want to be remembered for?

From the Playbook: Read Matthew 16:24–28.

TOP 25 GREAT BASKETBALL GAMES

THE PISTOL'S GREATEST GAME **February 25, 1977, New Orleans Jazz 124, New York Knicks 107**—For a Pete Maravich follower, it would be tempting to turn "25 Great Games" into "25 Great Moments for Pistol Pete." Finding his top game is not easy. But it just might be what he did to the New York Knicks while playing for the New Orleans Jazz. Guarded by defensive expert Walt Frazier, Maravich exploded for 68 points to help the Jazz win 124-107. He made 26 field goals and 16 free throws, and it's been estimated that if the NBA had used the three-point line in 1977, he would have tallied 80 points that night. Pistol Pete fouled out with 1:19 remaining in the game.

30. FIVE SUPERSTARS

Game Plan:
Working as a team

"A cord of three strands is not quickly broken."
ECCLESIASTES 4:12

An NBA story that took place a few years ago points out the value of teamwork. During the 2005–06 season, the Detroit Pistons got off to an incredible start. Also that season, in January, Kobe Bryant put together the second-greatest single-game scoring effort in NBA history with an 81-point performance.

But just a week after amassing that point total, Kobe and Co. had to face the Pistons in Detroit. Not surprisingly, Kobe canned quite a few shots and ended up scoring 39 points. He and Chris Mihm (16), however, were the only Los Angeles Lakers to score in double figures.

FAST FACT:

When Detroit beat LA 102-93 on January 29, 2006, the Pistons ran their record to an amazing 37-5 on the season.

The Pistons' team concept of basketball resulted in all five starters scoring in double figures as Detroit pounded LA in an impressive win. After the game, Detroit's Richard Hamilton said, "We feel as though we have five superstars."

When we go at it alone in life, it's difficult to be successful—either in our professional lives or our spiritual lives. Solomon described a greedy man in Ecclesiastes 4:7–8 who was "all alone." He was one miserable, discontented dude!

In contrast, the wise king described what happens when people walk and share with others (vv. 9–12). By teaming up, people will find that "a cord of three strands is not quickly broken."

Instead of trying to go it alone in life, seek out some fellow-believers who are of the same gender and mindset as you—men or women who want to grow in their relationship with Jesus. Meet with them consistently for a time of accountability, and you'll find that you found real strength as God works in and through all of you. —Tom Felten

FOLLOW THROUGH

Who are two or three people you could meet with consistently for accountability? Call them today and set up a time to meet together soon.

From the Playbook: Read Ecclesiastes 4:7–12.

GREAT BASKETBALL GAMES

KOBE GETS 81 January 22, 2006, Los Angeles Lakers 122, Toronto Raptors 104—Kobe Bryant can be unstoppable. Against the Raptors in mid-season 2006, he was so uncontainable that he came within 19 points of Wilt Chamberlain's all-time NBA scoring record. Bryant took 46 shots from the field and 20 from the line. He hit 60 percent from the field and 90 percent from the line. And he even took a six-minute break. He scored 26 in the first half, 27 in the third period, and 28 in the final quarter. The Lakers beat Toronto 122-104.

31. STAND TALL

Game Plan:
Overcoming our shortcomings

"There is no difference, for all have sinned and fall short of the glory of God." ROMANS 3:22–23

Imagine standing only 5-foot-5 and finding yourself playing in the NBA.

Welcome to Earl Boykins' world.

For 13 seasons, Boykins not only survived in the NBA but he was also for a while one of the league's top guards. During the 2006–07 season for the Denver Nuggets, he averaged just over 15 points a game, all while living in a basketball world ruled by the tall. Boykins never used his lack of height as a challenge, choosing to find promise in the talents God has given him to make his way to the basket time after time against obstacles like Yao Ming and Shaquille O'Neal.

FAST FACT:

Boykins is the second shortest player in NBA history behind 5'3" Muggsy Bogues.

How many times do we look at our lives and think—because of our sin—that we can't measure up to the person God wants us to be? We find ourselves comparing ourselves to others, thinking that because others have what we see as spiritual advantages, we can't make the most of the gifts God has bestowed upon us.

In Romans, Paul wrote that there is no difference. All of us—longtime Christians or new to the faith—deal with the same shortcomings. We all sin. All of us fail to live up to Christ's standards. But because of Jesus' sacrifice on the cross, we can stand tall, knowing that through God's grace, we are made new, earning us All-Star status in God's book.

—JEFF ARNOLD

FOLLOW THROUGH

The next time you find yourself tempted to think you can't live up to God's expectations, stop and pray. Ask Jesus to reveal His love to you and to give you a reminder that you belong to Him.

From the Playbook: Read Romans 3.

GREAT BASKETBALL GAMES

SPUD WINS SLAM DUNK **February 1986**—Okay, it's not a real game, but let's hear it for the little guys. In 1986, Spud Webb signed up for the NBA Slam Dunk Contest during the All-Star Break. This was a huge surprise to Dominique Wilkins, a classic dunker who had won the contest the previous year. He didn't even know Spud, his team-mate with the Atlanta Hawks, could throw it down. Since Webb was just 5' 7" tall, what else would Wilkins expect? But in the contest, Webb beat Wilkins with an array of slams that gave him a perfect score of 150 points—and an unlikely title for a little guy.

32. WHAT'S YOUR FOCAL POINT?

Game Plan:
Keeping focused on what is right

"Finally, brothers, whatever is true, whatever is noble, whatever is right, whatever is pure, whatever is lovely, whatever is admirable—if anything is excellent or praiseworthy—think about such things." PHILIPPIANS 4:8

There are so many distractions in life today! We feel as if we need to wake up and go, go, go! Our hurried lifestyles leave too little time for reflection about what we should be doing and what is right and wrong.

Too often, we let the corrupted everyday hustle and bustle stand in our way of the calm, soothing spirit of God. There are video games now that have such sexually explicit material or characters in them that it's no wonder there's a sexual struggle at an earlier age for kids. There's enough trash on TV anymore that if you don't flat out turn it off, it'll suck you right in to the "subliminal messages," potentially causing damage to marriages

It's not that all video games and television programs are bad (hey, the WNBA is on TV!), but we have to be careful what we fill our minds with. Paul wrote to Christians at Philippi and told them that "whatever is true, whatever is noble, whatever is right, whatever is pure, whatever is lovely... if anything is excellent or praiseworthy—think about such things" (Philippians 4:8).

FAST FACT:
Shanna Zolman married Andrew Crossley, a former football player at the University of Tennessee, on October 14, 2006.

What that means for us as it did for them is that we should "fix our eyes on the things from above." We shouldn't get so involved with what the world has to offer, because our treasures are not here on earth. Sure, God blesses us with things that will make our life here on earth more enjoyable, but those blessings should also be pleasing to Him.

What is noble in your life? What is pure or admirable? Whatever those things are that God has placed in your life, think and dwell upon them. Let them be the focal point of your mind instead of the negative ideas this world has to offer.

—SHANNA CROSSLEY

FOLLOW THROUGH

Think through some of the things you watch on TV. Can they be labeled noble, right, pure, and lovely?

From the Playbook: Read Philippians 4.

GREAT BASKETBALL GAMES

VILLANOVA DOESN'T MISS **April 1, 1985, Villanova 66, Georgetown 64**—Well, they didn't miss much from the field, and they certainly didn't miss their chance to upset the Georgetown Hoyas in the NCAA finals. Rollie Massimino's Wildcats put on a shooting clinic. The defending champion Hoyas were expected to repeat behind Patrick Ewing and a smothering defense. But somehow the Wildcats overcame that defense to put on one of the best shooting exhibitions ever. They shot 78 percent for the game, and astoundingly, they missed just one shot in the entire second half. Villanova upset Georgetown 66-64 to win the title.

33. THE BOND OF BASKETBALL— AND BEYOND

Game Plan:
Staying unified in Christ

"I appeal to you, brothers, ... that there may be no divisions among you." 1 CORINTHIANS 1:10

If you've never participated in a three-on-three basketball tournament, you've still got a lot of life to live. It's not just the nonstop basketball. There are people to watch, concession stands to raid, teams to admire.

While playing one summer in what was at the time the largest such tournament in the world—the Gus Macker 3-on-3 (4,400 teams, 18,000 players, 250,000 fans), I observed something else.

FAST FACT:
The first Gus Macker tournament was held in a driveway in 1974. Today it sponsors more than 50 tournaments across the US. Visit www .macker.com to find out more.

It's something Bob Becker, then the sports editor for the *Grand Rapids Press*, observed in an article he wrote about the tournament. "All weekend I see guys calling fouls on themselves and losers walking off courts with their arms around the shoulders of the winners. Most people up here don't know each other. But they all shoot hoops, and for most, that's enough." What Becker noticed was the bond of basketball. If you've played, you know what it means.

That kind of attitude should not be reserved for 3-on-3 basketball tournaments. It also should be the way believers in Christ get along. A reporter should be able to observe Christians in action and then say, "They love Jesus, and that's enough." Our common bond should be so strong that nothing can pull us apart.

Yet many things divide believers. Perhaps where you

worship there are divisions because of race or economic class. Maybe there are disagreements about church policy or something as ridiculous as the color of the carpet. It could be that people are going head-to-head about some theological question. Often those squabbles turn into heated, angry battles.

The Word of God suggests a better way. Like a bunch of people who get along because they love basketball, we need to be "perfectly united in mind and thought" because of our love for Jesus.

No matter what our background, we should be unified. Then others observing us can say, "They love Jesus, and that's enough."

—DAVE BRANON

FOLLOW THROUGH

What do you see dividing Christians in your church? Anything? If so, what can you do to turn the tide?

From the Playbook: Read 1 Corinthians 1:10–17.

TOP 25 GREAT BASKETBALL GAMES

BIRD VS. MAGIC, THE PREQUEL **March 26, 1979, Michigan State Spartans 75, Indiana State Sycamores 64**—It may not have been the best NCAA title game ever, but it was perhaps the most anticipated. And it was a precursor to what Larry Bird and Earvin Johnson would do later to help bring the NBA into the national consciousness as never before. Basketball fans everywhere got their first look at two intriguing superstars from neighboring states. Bird didn't have an especially good game, and Magic's Michigan State Spartans beat Bird's Indiana State Sycamores 75-64. But this was just the beginning, and Bird-Magic would become synonymous with basketball for the next 15 years and beyond.

34. SIGN ME UP!

Game Plan:
Recognizing the cost of discipleship

"The testing of your faith develops perseverance."
JAMES 1:3

My 8-year-old nephew returned from a father-son trip to the Palace of Auburn Hills pumped about his favorite team—the Detroit Pistons. As he was being tucked into bed a couple nights later, the young fella asked, "Dad, when I get older, could you sign me up for the NBA?" The only sports participation model he knew was YMCA soccer and basketball signups, so as far as he was concerned Tayshaun and the guys simply went down to the Palace with their parents and signed up to play. Then he asked, "Does it cost a lot to play in the NBA?"

FAST FACT:
How much does it cost to pay a team to play in the NBA? In 2009, it cost the Detroit Pistons about $77 million to pay their players.

Those two questions remind me of how I often react after reading Hebrews 11. Hebrews 11 is a list of people who had faith in God. There are familiar names like Noah, Abraham, and Moses, and there are unnamed believers who inspire me to trust God. If they had replica jerseys, I'd buy one. I read about them and I respond, "Sign me up to be a person of faith."

But I also need to know what I'm signing up for. I need to ask, "Does it cost a lot to be a person of faith?" According to Hebrews 11, it does. Each person listed developed faith during times of trials and hard times. Getting into the Faith Hall of Fame was not easy. Being a person of faith comes at a high cost.

So if you've "signed up" to be a person of faith by putting your trust in Jesus Christ to be your Savior and Lord, recognize that the difficulties you're experiencing in life are part of the program. While Jesus paid the price for your salvation, there still might be a cost to discipleship—of living for Jesus. Yet life's struggles are not sent your way to be hindrances to faith but to be opportunities for your faith to grow.

—BRIAN HETTINGA

FOLLOW THROUGH

Turn to Hebrews 11 in your Bible and sign your name at the top of the page. Then live today remembering that you've signed up to be a person of faith.

From the Playbook: Read Hebrews 11.

TOP 25 GREAT BASKETBALL GAMES

D IS NOT FOR DEFENSE December 13, 1983, **Detroit Pistons 186, Denver Nuggets 184**—December. Denver. Detroit. Lots of D's, but no D. On this remarkable NBA night, the Detroit Pistons beat the Denver Nuggets 186-184 in the highest scoring game in league history. In the ABA-like, high-scoring atmosphere of the 1980s, NBA teams scored with alacrity. Indeed, the Pistons averaged 117 points during the 1983–84 season. The Nuggets averaged even more: 123 points a game! And you thought the NBA didn't play defense these days! This game's total was helped by the fact that it was a triple-overtime contest. Here are some particulars. Twelve players hit double figures. Detroit had three guys over 30: Kelly Tripucka had 35, John Long had 41, and Isiah Thomas scored 47. Denver was led by Kiki Vandeweghe with 51 while Alex English notched 47. Nineteen players scored at least two points.

35. COOLER HEADS

> **Game Plan:**
> Handling problems well

"As far as it depends on you, live at peace with everyone."
ROMANS 12:18

During a time-out in a game between the New York Knicks and the Chicago Bulls in January 2006, Antonio Davis looked into the stands where his wife was sitting, and he noticed something wasn't right. For whatever reason, Mrs. Davis and a fan seemed to be having an argument.

Big No. 32 climbed over the press table and walked calmly toward his wife. After a few seconds, he discovered that things were under control, so he turned and walked away. Although he was protecting his wife and felt he had to take matters into his own hands for her good, the NBA suspended him for five games for going into the stands—a clear violation of player rules.

But then came the aftermath. The word "lawsuit" was tossed around by the fan. The figure "$1 million" was mentioned. It looked as if this incident was going to get really ugly. Lawyers. Courtroom arguments. Endless press coverage. It had all the trappings of a sports soap opera.

But then cooler heads prevailed. Both sides actually got together and talked to each other. And in the end they released a joint statement that said, in part, "common sense strongly suggests that we collectively put this episode behind us and move on."

How many times in life would we all be so much better off if we were to use that bit of wisdom? How many grudges could we drop if we were to talk things out with the person we disagree with? How many offended people could understand more clearly? How many angry decisions would we avoid?

Here's how the apostle Paul put it as he spoke God's inspired message: "As far as it depends on you, live at peace with everyone" (Romans 12:18). When anger brews, let's honor God's wishes for us and let cooler heads prevail.

—DAVE BRANON

FOLLOW THROUGH

What situation that I am facing right now could be solved if I would strive to "live at peace"? What should I do about it?

From the Playbook: Read Romans 12:9–21.

TOP 25 GREAT BASKETBALL GAMES

BAYLOR BURIES 61 **April 14, 1962, Los Angeles Lakers 125, Boston Celtics 121**—Elgin Baylor was a scoring machine that not even the likes of Satch Sanders and Bill Russell could stop. In Game 5 of the 1962 NBA finals, the Lakers' forward scored 61 points to set a record for the Finals that still stands today. Only Michael Jordan's 63 points has topped Baylor's mark in overall playoffs history. Baylor also picked up 22 rebounds as the Lakers beat the Celtics 125-121 at the famed Boston Garden.

36. NOT ENOUGH

Game Plan:
Knowing what is truly important

"All his days his work is pain and grief; even at night his mind does not rest. This too is meaningless."
ECCLESIASTES 2:23

Mike Davis had one of the top coaching jobs in the country. For six years, Davis was the leader of Indiana University men's basketball team. Few NCAA schools have the rich tradition of Hoosiers basketball. Fewer still had such high expectations for its team than the Hoosiers did at the time Davis became coach.

Davis, who took over the program immediately following the dismissal of ultra-popular head coach Bob Knight in 2000, led Indiana to the 2002 NCAA championship game. He guided the Hoosiers to a 115-79 record during his tenure. Yet it wasn't enough for many fans in this basketball-crazy state. On February 15, 2006, Mike Davis resigned as Indiana's basketball coach. He finished the remainder of the season and coached the Hoosiers in the NCAA tournament.

FAST FACT:

Mike Davis played college basketball at the University of Alabama. In 2006, he became the head coach at the University of Alabama-Birmingham.

At the time of Davis' resignation, Tamilya Davis told the Associated Press, "I think my husband's had enough of the limelight."

The prestige. The money. The attention. All the perks and accolades that come with Indiana basketball were not enough to sustain Mike Davis, a strong Christian who knows that there is so much more to life than trying to keep an army of alumni and students happy.

In Ecclesiastes, another man found similar realities in

life's pursuits. Riches, pleasure, power—the teacher of Ecclesiastes declared them all meaningless. What does man gain from hard work, from the pursuit of riches, or from the chasing after knowledge? The teacher writes that nothing was worthy of man's time and energy apart from a life with a healthy fear of God and a yearning to honor Him by following His commandments.

Seeking all that the world has to offer is simply not enough to sustain. Only a strong relationship with God can do that.

—ROB BENTZ

FOLLOW THROUGH

Spend a few moments examining your own life. Ask yourself, what am I pursuing in this life to make me feel happy/comfortable/significant? Then read Ecclesiastes 12:9–14 to gain a biblical perspective.

From the Playbook: Read Ecclesiastes 2:17–27 and 12:9–14.

TOP 25 GREAT BASKETBALL GAMES

LAETTNER SCORES! **March 28, 1992, Duke Blue Devils 104, Kentucky Wildcats 103**—The magic of this game-ending shot was not just the shot itself. It was all that led up to it, including the fact that defending champ Duke was playing perennial power Kentucky. But there was also the roller coaster of the previous 29 seconds of the overtime. First Christian Laettner scored to make it 100-98. Then Jamal Mashburn scored and was fouled. Now it was 101-100. Mashburn fouled Laettner, who hit two to make it 102-101. Sean Woods hit a shot, and it was 103-102 Kentucky with just 2.1 seconds left. You know what happened next. Grant Hill heaved a three-quarter-length pass to Laettner, who turned and fired the ball through the net and Duke won 104-103. And everybody collapsed in exhaustion. Fans included.

37. STEVE NASH'S EGO

Game Plan:
Working for the good of the church

"There are many parts, but one body."
1 CORINTHIANS 12:20

In May 2006, Phoenix Suns guard Steve Nash joined an elite group of basketball players who had won the league MVP trophy two years in a row. This was an unlikely achievement for a man from a country known more for producing hockey players.

Nash, who was born in South Africa but grew up as a Canadian citizen, wasn't even recruited out of high school by any Division I colleges from the United States. Despite being the player of the year in British Columbia after his high school senior year, Nash had to convince Santa Clara University to take a look at him. Once Santa Clara's coach Dick Davey saw him play, he immediately knew he had stumbled onto a special talent.

FAST FACT:
Nash led No. 15 seed Santa Clara to an upset win over No. 2 seed Arizona in the first round of the 1993 NCAA Tournament.

After Nash's college career ended, the Phoenix Suns selected Nash with their 15th pick in the first round of the 1996 NBA Draft. He was eventually traded to Dallas, where he played well. But it wasn't until he returned to the Suns at the age of 30 that he really began to shine. In his first season back, he led Phoenix to 62 wins and earned his first MVP award.

When asked if winning a second MVP award would go to his head, Nash said, "Everyone has ego. The trick is to learn how to use ego for the good of the team."

I love that response! That's exactly the kind of humility and unity communities of Christians need to further God's kingdom. Although Christians have different levels of talent, we make up one unit that is meant to work together for a greater good (1 Corinthians 12:12).

If God's kingdom is to move forward, rather than around in circles, we must not forget that the whole is always greater than the sum of its parts (1 Corinthians 12:21–25). We need to work "for the good of the team." Is that the kind of ego you have?   —JEFF OLSON

FOLLOW THROUGH

Is there a place in your Christian life where success has gone to your head? What should your attitude be toward the talents and responsibilities God has given you?

For Further Study: Check out www.discoveryseries.org and read the booklet *Who Qualifies to Be a Church Leader?*

TOP 25 GREAT BASKETBALL GAMES

A TECHNICAL KNOCKOUT **June 4, 1976, Boston Celtics 128, Phoenix Suns 126**—The fun began in overtime as Boston and Phoenix battled in Game 5 of the NBA Finals. In the first extra session, the score was tied as time ran down. Boston's Paul Silas signaled a time-out—which Boston didn't have. The officials ignored the signal, and Phoenix was incensed. They should have been at the line shooting a technical foul. Instead, they went into a second overtime. With four seconds left in OT and the Suns leading 110-109, John Havlicek scored. Fans poured onto the court, thinking the Celtics had won. Several minutes later, after order was restored, there was one second left. The Suns' Paul Westphal had a plan. Call a time-out the Suns didn't have. That would put the Celtics at the line for one shot, but the Suns would get the ball out at half court. It worked. Boston hit their shot, but the Suns got a miracle shot from Gar Heard to tie the game and send it to a third OT. Boston won in 3 OTs 128-126.

38. DRIVING A DIFFERENT LANE

Game Plan:
Working for others

"Each of you should look not only to your own interests, but also to the interests of others." PHILIPPIANS 2:4

Chris Paul has certainly made a name for himself as an NBA All-Star, but he insists (maybe with tongue firmly implanted in cheek) that hoops is not his main game. "I tell people all the time that I do basketball as a hobby. Bowling is what I really do."

The young man from Winston-Salem, North Carolina, a sponsored spokesman for the United States Bowling Congress, organized a bowling tournament in his hometown one summer to help raise money so that local students could attend Wake Forest, his alma mater. Who hit the lanes with CP3? A bunch of basketball buddies including LeBron James, Dwyane Wade, Carmelo Anthony, and Dwight Howard.

FAST FACT:
Chris Paul averaged nearly 20 points a game through the first five years of his NBA career.

The scholarship Chris established at Wake Forest is named for his grandfather, Nathaniel Jones, who was murdered when the young NBA star was still in high school. Family is important to Paul. In fact, his family introduced him to bowling and gave him his first ball as a Christmas present when he was in his early teens. Now he's rolling strikes to help others.

Have you ever thought about how you can use your talents and hobbies to help others? It's easy to let our interests become purely self-interests instead of sacrificially using our interests to glorify God.

In Philippians 2, the apostle Paul addresses the selfish ways that had surfaced in the church at Philippi. He implored the believers to "consider others better than yourselves" (v. 3). Pride and selfishness can keep us from doing just that, but when we're full of ourselves and not interested in helping others, we're also showing a lack of humility and devotion before God.

What talents and interests can you use this week to enrich someone's life? Consider Chris Paul's example and use your "game" for the good of others! —TOM FELTEN

FOLLOW THROUGH

Pray and ask God to reveal to you how you can use your talents and interests to bless others and glorify Him. Before engaging in your activities this week, ask, "How can I use this interest to bless others?"

From the Playbook: Read Philippians 2:1–11.

TOP 25

GREAT BASKETBALL GAMES

A BULL MARKET **April 20, 1986, Boston Celtics 135, Chicago Bulls 131**—Michael Jordan was beginning to be seen for what he could be—one of the greatest players in the NBA. But his Chicago Bulls were still not quite ready for prime time. However, in the midst of getting swept by the Celtics in the 1986 playoffs, Jordan served notice. His time was coming. In the greatest playoff performance in NBA history, MJ scored 63 points against the Celtics in Game 2, which was won by Boston 135-131. It was a moment in Jordan's career that hinted of great things to come.

39. ORIGINAL RULES FOR SALE

Game Plan:
Living by God's standards

"Hold firmly to the trustworthy message as it has been taught." TITUS 1:9

A few years ago, the folks who owned the original 13 rules for the game of basketball put them up for sale—for $10 million!

In 1891 Dr. James A. Naismith invented the game of basketball and drafted the rules. Although those rules stayed locked away in storage for 115 years, the game of basketball is being played by young and old on courts all over the world—and using a rulebook that ballooned from Naismith's original 500 words to the 30,000 words it takes today to control the game! Back in 2005, Naismith's grandson, Ian Naismith, decided to try to sell the rules for $10 million, with the proceeds going to fund the Naismith International Basketball Foundation. And eventually, Ian hopes, the rules will be put on display at the Smithsonian Institution.

FAST FACT:
Naismith's Rule No. 5: "No shouldering, holding, pushing, tripping, or striking ... an opponent."

Those first 13 rules were the basis for the game as we know it today. Without Naismith's foresight in creating practical rules for the game he invented on a cold Massachusetts night in the winter of 1891, the game would never have achieved its place in sports lore.

Yet far more important than this $10 million set of rules is something you can get in a book for under $10. It's the written Word of God. Most people call it the Bible. Penned over a long period of time more than 2,000 years ago, this Book was intended to give us the "rules" for the game of life—including the No. 1 Rule: "Believe in the Lord Jesus, and you will be saved" (Acts 16:31).

However, over time many people have lost respect and reverence for the Bible. In 1963, according to a Gallup poll, 65 percent of Americans believed the Bible literally; today that number is 32 percent. Overall, our knowledge of biblical truth is on the decline.

How are you doing with God's standards, which are so readily available? Are the "original rules" from God's Book up for sale in your life?   —MOLLY RAMSEYER

FOLLOW THROUGH

Ask God if you have changed the rules in your life? Commit anew today to revere and obey scriptural commands.

From the Playbook: Read Colossians 3:16, Hebrews 4:12, Isaiah 34:16, and Isaiah 30:9.

TOP 25 GREAT BASKETBALL GAMES

THE SHOT **June 14, 1998, Chicago Bulls 87, Utah Jazz 86—** With Scottie Pippen suffering a bad back, Michael Jordan had to take matters into his own hands to avoid going back to Chicago for Game 7 of the 1998 NBA Finals. The Bulls led the Utah Jazz 3-2 heading into the game. Late in the contest, John Stockton knocked down a three-pointer, and the Jazz led 86-83. Jordan scored on a lay-up to make it a one-point game. Then he stole a Stockton pass and dribbled into the frontcourt. With Byron Russell guarding him, Jordan executed a crossover, gave Russell a little no-call shove, rose into the air, and drilled home a deuce to put the Bulls on top 87-86 with 5.2 seconds left. When a Stockton triple-try bounced off the iron, the Bulls were again the NBA champs, and Michael Jordan had played his last game in a Chicago uniform, finishing his Windy City career with 45 points, another Finals MVP trophy, and one more NBA championship.

40. THE GREAT JIMMY V.

Game Plan:
Planning for the inevitable

"There is now no condemnation for those who are in Christ Jesus." ROMANS 8:1

Jim Valvano was 21 years old and ready to take the court for his first coaching job as the mentor of the Rutgers freshman basketball team. For his pregame pep talk, Valvano had memorized a brief speech from the mind of venerable Green Bay Packers coach Vince Lombardi.

Perhaps it should have been briefer.

First, Coach Valvano tried to barge through the locker room door like Lombardi, but it didn't open immediately and he hurt his arm. Once he got in front of his guys, he paced back and forth before them before saying, as dramatically as he could, "Gentlemen, we'll be successful this year if you can focus on three things, and three things only: Your family, your religion, and the Green Bay Packers."

The Packers?

Twenty-six years later, on March 3, 1993, Jimmy V. made another speech, this one at the first-ever ESPY Awards. Everyone knew the longtime coach at North Carolina State (national champions, 1983) was dying of cancer, and Valvano spoke his mind: "Cancer can take away all my physical ability. It cannot touch my mind; it cannot touch my heart; and it cannot touch my soul. And those three things are going to carry on forever."

Less than two months later, beloved basketball coach Jim Valvano was dead.

FAST FACT:

Jim Valvano and Dick Vitale made a cameo appearance together on The Cosby Show. They were furniture movers in an episode called "The Getaway."

We all face an inevitable departure from this world. And we will spend forever in one of two realms—either with God in heaven or separated from Him in hell. That should cause us to consider what He says about us.

Because we all sin (Romans 3:23), we all fail God. Thankfully, we can be "justified freely by his grace through the redemption that came by Christ Jesus" (v. 24). Therefore, we need to ask God the Father for His gracious forgiveness, available to us through His Son. Because of Jesus' death and resurrection, we don't have to fear death. We can carry on forever with Him!

—TIM GUSTAFSON

FOLLOW THROUGH

Are you hoping that you've been "good enough" for God to let you into heaven? What does Romans 3:10–12 say about such a false hope? Have you ever asked God for His forgiveness?

From the Playbook: Read Romans 3:21–26.

TOP 25 GREAT BASKETBALL GAMES

REGGIE BEATS NY, PART 1   June 1, 1994, Indiana Pacers 93, New York Knicks 86—A legendary rivalry was born this day when Reggie Miller took on the New York Knicks, the fans at Madison Square Garden, and Spike Lee in an amazing display of shooting prowess and fan-player interaction. It was Game 5 of the Eastern Conference Finals. Miller had 14 points as the teams headed into the fourth quarter, and that's when the fun began. Reggie scored 25 points in that stanza, including several three-pointers. In the midst of this scoring blitz, Miller and Lee, who was seated courtside, partook in an animated display of two-way trash talk. It was an entertaining quarter, and the Indiana Pacers had the last laugh, winning 93-86.

41. SETTING UP SOME EXPECTATIONS

> **Game Plan:**
> Realizing your ultimate goals

"In his heart a man plans his course, but the Lord determines his steps." PROVERBS 16:9

Goals are an integral part of an athlete's life. It seems that everyone asks an athlete "What are your goals for this season?" Or "What are your goals for your career?"

Short-term and long-term performance-oriented goals are the rage. Goals are encouraged, measured, promoted, and evaluated to no end in the lives of athletes.

Do we as Christians have goals? We should. No. 1 in our lives should be to come into fellowship with the Lord our God. Did you know that it is for this purpose alone that we have been created? It is only in our fellowship with God that we can find our ultimate significance, understand our true meaning, and find our life dreams fulfilled. A win in sports lasts for a moment in time. Our fellowship with the Lord will last us for eternity.

For 6 long years at Kansas State we lost miserably before we won. In 2003 we won a Big 12 championship. Regardless of our early struggles, we lived and competed in the incredible grace and blessing of God—seeking the eternal prize, not just momentary glory.

Sports provide us with an opportunity to express the gifts and abilities God has given and blessed us with. Ephesians 1:18 and 19 declares, "That you may know the hope to which he has called you, the riches of his glorious inheritance in the saints, and his incomparably great power for us who believe." God gives us the power to live for His glory. It is only in knowing God and living for Him that we walk in the steps He has ultimately created for us to follow.

What is our ultimate goal? What are our greatest expectations? To know and love the Lord with all our heart and soul and mind and strength (Mark 12:30). —DEB PATTERSON

FOLLOW THROUGH

If your No. 1 goal is bringing glory to God through your relationship with Him, what might be a couple of secondary goals you can set for yourself?

From the Playbook: Read Proverbs 16:1–7.

TOP 25
GREAT BASKETBALL GAMES

REGGIE BEATS NY, PART II   May 7, 1995, Indiana Pacers 107, New York Knicks 105—Reggie Miller led the Indiana Pacers in another fourth-quarter blitz against the NY Knicks (as he had done in 1994), but this time he did his damage in an incredibly short time. With 16.4 seconds left in Game 1 of the Eastern Conference semifinals, New York led by six points. In the next 8.9 seconds, Miller scored 8 points. He hit a three, stole the inbounds pass and stepped back for another three. The Knicks' John Starks was fouled on the next inbounds play. He missed both free throws, Patrick Ewing missed a put-back, Miller rebounded, was fouled, and made two free throws—and the Pacers won 107-105.

42. J WILL'S DEFERRED DREAM

Game Plan:
Hoping in God in the face of trouble

"You have been my hope, O Sovereign Lord, my confidence since my youth." Psalm 71:5

The NBA future looked bright for Jay Williams, the 2002 Naismith College Player of the Year and John R. Wooden Award recipient, who played for Mike Krzyzewski at Duke.

He was selected No. 2 in the NBA draft and played one season for the Chicago Bulls. But a devastating motorcycle accident in the summer of 2003 put a dent in his NBA dream. His injuries included a severed main nerve in his leg, fractured pelvis, and three torn ligaments in his left knee.

After a long period of rehabilitation, Williams signed a non-guaranteed contract with the New Jersey Nets in September 2006. However, things didn't work out, and he was released by his hometown Nets in October (he went to high school in Metuchen, New Jersey).

FAST FACT:
During his rookie season, Williams posted one triple-double for the Chicago Bulls—against the New Jersey Nets.

Jay had worked hard to get back to playing ball, but it was just not to be. Sadly, his NBA dream had been deferred.

Perhaps you can identify with Jay. Most of us have dreams that have vanished in the light of life's harsh realities. But even when our ultimate dreams don't come true, there is still hope.

An unnamed psalmist once wrote, "I have become like a portent to many" (71:7). He was viewed as a sign of trouble, and people disliked him. This old man could have felt like his life dreams were history.

Instead, he chose to trust God. He refused to let go of hope because of his faith in his "Sovereign Lord," who had been his "confidence since . . . youth" (v. 5).

Are you feeling down for the count? Take heart. The all-powerful God of the universe can guide you through your difficulties and deferred dreams. Choose to place your hope in Him today.   —TOM FELTEN

FOLLOW THROUGH

Write down several of your dreams for this life. Take them to God in prayer and give them to Him. Close by telling Him that He is your hope!

From the Playbook: Read Psalm 71.

TOP 25 GREAT BASKETBALL GAMES

TERPS BEDEVILED BY DUKE   **March 31, 2001, Duke Blue Devils 95, Maryland Terrapins 84**—In the first game of this national semifinal contest, the Maryland Terrapins raced out to a 39-17 first half lead before Duke cut the lead to 11, 49-38, at the half. Maryland maintained a comfortable lead as the game wound down to the final minutes. In fact, with just 54 seconds to play, the Terps held a cushy 10-point margin. In the next 34 seconds, Duke ate up that 10-point lead. Maryland had the ball with 20 seconds left but didn't get a shot off—and the game went into overtime. It was all Duke in OT, as they won 95-84.

43. PLAYING LIKE THE PISTOL

Game Plan:
Following good examples

"Dear friend, do not imitate what is evil but what is good." 3 JOHN 11

As much as I appreciated my college basketball coach for everything he taught me as a spiritual mentor, there was one thing we did not agree on. He didn't like my imitation of Pete Maravich—the greatest showman in college hoops history. My coach was old school. I, on the other hand, was a member of the "Let's make this game as much fun as we can" club. That's why I spent so much time practicing Pistol Pete's fancy moves. From spinning the ball on my finger to throwing no-look passes to firing jumpers from way, way downtown, I tried every Maravich move I could conjure up.

FAST FACT:

In 83 games during his college career, Pete Maravich scored fewer than 30 points just four times. He had 50 or more points in a game 24 times during his three seasons at LSU.

But I know my coach was really ticked at me during one game when I put together a between-the-legs then behind-the-back bounce pass while on a fast break. Flying full-speed down the court, I dribbled the ball between my legs from my right hand to my left, then cradled the ball in my left hand, and flipped it behind my back to the man coming down the court in the right lane. It was a thing of absolute hoops beauty.

As I sat on the bench a moment later contemplating my love for fancy passes, I got an earful from Mr. Old School. To him, my imitation of one of the Pistol's patented moves was an imitation of evil. He preferred that I imitate something good—like a boring, old two-handed bounce pass.

In real life, imitation of true evil is far more serious. When we choose to follow the lead of someone who is influencing us to do something that violates God's standards, we disobey God. Conversely, 3 John 11 says, "Anyone who does what is good is from God."

Knowing whom to imitate isn't easy. But one set of questions can guide our choices: Does this person make godly choices? Stand for what is right? Care what God thinks? If so, that person is someone you can follow.

Think of your influences: media, friends, music, even sports. Which are you imitating? The good or the evil?

—DAVE BRANON

FOLLOW THROUGH

What are your standards for what is good? Can you find a biblical basis for your guidelines?

From the Playbook: Read 3 John 11.

TOP 25 GREAT BASKETBALL GAMES

OLD-SCHOOL HOOPS   March 23, 1957, North Carolina Tar Heels 54, Kansas Jayhawks 53—The 1957 NCAA championship game pitted Frank McGuire's North Carolina Tar Heels against Kansas and its huge center from Philadelphia, Wilt Chamberlain. The game was marked by a confrontation between the players as both benches emptied in the first overtime when the Heels fouled Chamberlain hard. Police had to usher the fans back to their seats so play could resume. The Jayhawks led by one, 53-52 as the clock wound down in the third overtime. Chamberlain blocked two shots, but North Carolina's Joe Quigg picked up a loose ball and was fouled. With six seconds left, he sank both free throws, and Carolina won 54-53.

44. GETTING FIT

Game Plan:
Gaining spiritual fitness

"Man looks at the outward appearance, but the Lord looks at the heart." 1 SAMUEL 16:7

In 1988, at the age of 40, one of my personal heroes, "Pistol Pete" Maravich—one of the greatest basketball players of all time—died while playing a pickup game in California. Maravich was a health freak whose last words were, "I'm really feeling good."

On the day he died, Pete Maravich had the external appearance of exceptional physical health. He was young. He was still slender. He seemed to be in playing shape.

FAST FACT:
Pete Maravich scored 3,667 points in college and 15,948 in the NBA.

But he had an unseen, congenital, fatal heart problem. He appeared to be a model of physical fitness, but his well-conditioned body had hidden a serious sickness his entire life. It was a problem that he had carried with him unawares through four remarkable years at LSU and 10 outstanding years in the NBA.

This kind of thing can happen to us spiritually as well. The religious world is often stunned when someone perceived to be spiritually healthy is exposed as spiritually diseased. Spiritual sickness often looks like fitness, because we are trained to evaluate fitness by a set of superficial standards. Symptoms of spiritual sickness, masked by religious behavior, often are undetected.

David begged God to create within him a clean, pure, righteous heart (Psalm 51:10). Why? Because David knew that the heart of man is deceitfully wicked and stubborn—concerned only with gratifying self.

So, are you ready to get FIT? Fit on the inside? Here's a plan:

- God desires us to be *faithful*—not famous! It's His name—not ours that is to be magnified.
- He commands that we *invest* in the lives of others—not *isolated* and consumed with self.
- Our Father wants us *teachable*—not a *theological know-it-all.*

Do you have a passion for God? Does your heart cry for intimacy with Him? Then get FIT. Be *faithful*. Begin *investing* in others. Be *teachable*. And see what a pure heart can do for Him!

—Tim Cash

FOLLOW THROUGH

Rate yourself from 1 to 10 on faithfulness, investing, and teachability. How can you get better at those things as you strive to be more FIT?

From the Playbook: Read Psalm 51.

TOP 25 GREAT BASKETBALL GAMES

ADAM'S TEARS   **March 23, 2006, UCLA Bruins 73, Gonzaga Bulldogs 71**—What could have been Adam Morrison's finest moment became his worst defeat. College basketball's player of the year had led his Gonzaga Bulldogs to a nine-point lead over the UCLA Bruins in the regional semifinals. Just three minutes stood between the Zags and the Elite Eight. Morrison hit two free throws at the 3:27 mark to give the Bulldogs a 71-62 lead. Then UCLA scored the game's final 11 points to win 73-71, and Morrison was reduced to tears as he lay on the floor of the arena. It was his last college basketball game.

45. THE BEST LEGACY

"If what he has built survives, he will receive his reward."
1 CORINTHIANS 3:14

The enduring image of Red Auerbach, the peerless Boston Celtics coach of the 1950s and 1960s, will be of him sitting on the sideline, brazenly enjoying a victory cigar while his players put the finishing touches on another win.

Auerbach, who died in 2006 at age 89, is pro basketball's greatest coaching icon. Arnold Auerbach's first pro coaching stint came in the old Basketball Association of America, where he skippered the Washington Capitals and the Tri-Cities Blackhawks. But in 1950, he became the head man in Boston. Before he was through, he had coached Boston to an unprecedented nine NBA championships in 10 years and presided over another six as general manager. Celtics Hall of Famer Bill Russell called Auerbach "the best coach in the history of professional sports, period."

FAST FACT:
Auerbach played college basketball at George Washington University from 1938 through 1941.

That's quite a legacy!

Legacies are important. But it's best not to reserve them for our personal glory. We want to leave a good legacy for spiritual reasons. While our salvation is not based on works—the great passage in Ephesians 2:8–9 tells us that—look at what the next verse says, "For we are God's workmanship, created in Christ Jesus to do good works, which God prepared in advance for us to do."

The Bible makes it clear that our earthly deeds will carry weight in eternity. First Corinthians 3:12–15 and Revelation

3:16 provide stern warnings for do-nothing Christians. One of the main themes of the book of James is the importance of our tangible spiritual efforts.

One day, each of us will face a comprehensive life evaluation in heaven as we stand before the throne of the Lord God Almighty (Revelation 20:12). That's a sobering picture, but if we're faithful, we will hear, "Well done, good and faithful servant."

That's the best legacy of all. —Joshua Cooley

FOLLOW THROUGH

Take an inventory of your spiritual gift(s) and how effectively you are using them. If you don't know what they are, pray for God to reveal them and, if needed, seek the counsel of a pastor or trusted spiritual mentor.

From the Playbook: Read Matthew 25:14–30.

TOP 25 GREAT BASKETBALL GAMES

THE CELTICS' DYNASTY BEGINS **April 13, 1957, Boston Celtics 125, St. Louis Hawks 123**—Back in a time when the NBA Finals finished before the major league baseball season began (April 16, 1957), the Boston Celtics were getting their first taste of championship basketball. Game 7 of the 1957 Finals pitted Boston against the St. Louis Hawks. The Celtics were led by Tommy Heinsohn, who scored 37 points and grabbed 23 rebounds. He got big-time help from fellow rookie Bill Russell, who blocked five shots, scored 19 points, and ripped down 32 rebounds. Good thing. The backcourt of Bill Sharman and Bob Cousy went 5-for-40. The Celtics needed two overtimes to get by the Hawks 125-123.

46. LESSONS FROM THE WATERBOYS

Game Plan:
Making living water available

"Whoever drinks the water I give him will never thirst."
JOHN 4:14

Sometimes when I go to high school basketball games and I see elementary kids handing out water to the players, I think, "What's this? Can't the players stand up and get their own water? Do we need 11-year-olds waiting on 17-year-olds?"

FAST FACT:

Former baseball commissioner Bowie Kuhn was a batboy for the Washington Senators as a kid. Rapper MC Hammer was a batboy for the Oakland A's as a youngster—when he was still Stanley Burrell.

But then I think of the benefits. For the players, it is vital to stay hydrated during the game, and having the kids continually handing them cups of water reminds them to drink—something they might not otherwise do because they are either listening to the coach or concentrating on the game. (Okay, or scanning the stands to find their friends.) But I decided that the younger kids also gain from being waterboys. They are developing a servant's heart by helping others.

Handing out water to the thirsty is something Jesus demonstrated in John 4. The difference between what the water boys do and what Jesus did was that Jesus was giving out "living water." He was distributing more than something to take away thirst—He was distributing something that could take away sin.

As Jesus and the Samaritan woman stood by the well where they had met while seeking good old H_2O, Jesus told the woman, "whoever drinks the water I give him will never thirst"(John 4:14). This "water," which we know to represent

104

the eternal life that comes through faith in Christ, was the only thing that could rescue this woman from her state of spiritual dryness.

She accepted Jesus' offer and even went into her town to tell others where to find the "water."

Got any thirsty friends? Friends who are dying for a drink of living water? It takes a servant to make sure they get it. Like the waterboys are with the players, be willing to distribute the living water to those who need it. —DAVE BRANON

FOLLOW THROUGH

Which of your friends are thirsty spiritually? How can you get them the living water without alienating or offending them?

From the Playbook: Read John 4:1–15.

TOP 25 GREATEST BASKETBALL GAMES

MAGIC IN THE MIDDLE   Game 6, 1980, Los Angeles Lakers 123, Philadelphia 76ers 107—How often does an NBA point guard get to play center? Not often, but when he's 6'9" tall and one of the greatest players ever, it can happen. In Game 5 of the NBA Finals between the Lakers and the 76ers, LA's big man, Kareem Abdul-Jabbar, sprained his ankle. In Game 6, Earvin "Magic" Johnson filled in for him. And he dominated. Magic scored 42 points, snared 15 rebounds, and dished out seven assists. The Lakers won 123-107, and Magic added another page to his legend.

47. NO PAIN, NO GAIN

Game Plan:
Persevering during the hard times

"We are heirs—heirs of God and co-heirs with Christ, if indeed we share in his sufferings." ROMANS 8:17

Imagine playing for a professional basketball team whose fans always expect nothing from you.

Welcome to Chris Kaman's world. In 2003, Kaman was drafted into the NBA by the Los Angeles Clippers, a team that, in 2006, won its first playoff series in 29 years. Just 6 years earlier, the Clippers had won only 15 of 82 games, continuing a long tradition of being considered one of the NBA's worst franchises.

FAST FACT:

After his high school career at tiny Tri-Unity Christian High School in Grand Rapids, Michigan, Chris Kaman was recruited by only two colleges: Division III Hope College and Central Michigan. He chose Central Michigan.

But Kaman, who made the All-Star team in 2010, his seventh year with the team, was drafted as part of a rebuilding process that required patience and hard work, but one that eventually led to that 2006 playoff run. His entire Clippers career has been one of a few ups and a lot of downs.

This is a little like what happens in our Christian lives. We know that we have a heavenly reward waiting for us because we've put our faith in Jesus. But along the way we're going to have seasons when not much goes right—times when we wonder when it's going to be our time to enjoy some good news.

Sure, there will be times when God brings us joy, but it's never guaranteed. In Romans 8, we learn that being part of God's family means that we must sometimes suffer as Jesus did before we can share in His glory (v. 17). Jesus experienced a lot of suffering when He was here on earth, and He endured ridicule and mocking—all as part of the process of being sent to the cross to die for our sins. So, now He's calling us to live through some suffering while we wait for the eternal joys that have been promised to us in heaven.

It's all part of the process that God has for us.

So, when things do go just as you want them to, remember: You're an heir of God.

—JEFF ARNOLD

FOLLOW THROUGH

If you're currently going through a tough season of life, God has a purpose in bringing you through it. Maybe He's asking for more faith on your part or maybe He wants to see if you'll continue to be a testimony for Him even in difficult times. Why not seek out God and try and discover what He has for you in this time.

From the Playbook: Read Romans 8.

TOP 25 GREAT BASKETBALL GAMES

WILLIS REED RETURNS   **May 9, 1970, New York Knicks 113, Los Angeles Lakers 99**—More than 40 years after it happened, Willis Reed's hobbling return to the Madison Square Garden court still inspires all who saw it unfold. The LA Lakers and the New York Knicks had returned to the Garden for Game 7 of the NBA Finals. Reed had not played for a couple of games as he nursed his injured knee. As the teams came out to warm up for Game 7, no Willis Reed was in sight. In fact, he was in the locker room, where team doctors were giving him shots to numb the pain. With just five minutes to go before tip-off, big No. 19 slowly and painfully made his way through the tunnel and out onto the floor as nearly 20,000 fans went crazy. Reed's presence lifted the Knicks, and they conquered the Lakers 113-99.

48. JIMMY CHITWOOD'S JUMPER

Game Plan:
Remaining true to Jesus

"What she has done will also be told, in memory of her." MARK 14:9

In the classic basketball movie *Hoosiers*, Jimmy Chitwood was a star. In real life, the actor who portrayed him never played high school basketball. Maris Valainis' high school game was truly forgettable. Every year he went out for the team. Every year he got cut. Yet despite losing out on his dream, Maris Valainis kept practicing.

Even after high school, Maris continued to play the game he loved. One day a casting director for *Hoosiers* spotted him dropping jumpers from all over the floor at an elementary gym. He became the only Hickory High School actor/player who did not play high school hoops in real life. Now his picture-perfect jumper is the memory we recall when we think of mythical Hickory High winning the 1951 Indiana State High School championship game. And to think the hero never played basketball in high school.

FAST FACT:
While filming Hoosiers, *Wade Schenck, who played Ollie, had to shoot under-handed free throws because his regular free throws were too smooth for the character of a manager-turned-player.*

Sometimes, our spiritual life can be kind of like Valainis and his effort to make the high school basketball team. He never made it to his goal, but he didn't stop getting better. And we should never give up when it comes to Bible-reading and talking with God—even if we don't reach the level we have in mind.

Valainis didn't know it when he was practicing all those hours, but he was getting ready to do something that would be remembered for a long time. Think of that in regard to the woman in Mark 14. She had no idea that her simple act of kindness toward Jesus would be remembered 2,000 years later. Yet her memory lives on because of her actions and her complete loyalty to Christ.

Don't you give up. Keep learning about, reading about, and talking with Jesus Christ. Then stay ready for God to use you in a memorable way. —DAN DEAL

FOLLOW THROUGH

What spiritual discipline is your biggest challenge? How can you keep it going strong in your life?

From the Playbook: Read the story of the unnamed woman in Mark 14:1–9 or Matthew 26:6–12. Proverbs 37 is filled with purpose for your life.

TOP 25 GREAT BASKETBALL GAMES

GAME OF THE CENTURY MARK **March 2, 1962, Philadelphia Warriors 169, New York Knicks 145**—Adrian Monk would have liked this. While tallying the highest point total in NBA history by one player in a game, Wilt Chamberlain accumulated a nice, even 100 points. And he did it by doing something he rarely did: by hitting free throws. The big man for the Philadelphia Warriors led his team past the New York Knicks 169-145. He hit 28 free throws in 32 attempts—far exceeding his career mark of right around 50 percent. He took 63 shots from the field and hit 36. The game was played in Hershey, Pennsylvania.

49. GAME-CLOCK MATH

Game Plan:
Understanding God's timing

"With the Lord a day is like a thousand years and a thousand years are like a day." 2 PETER 3:8

Honey, when are you coming to bed?" a wife asks her husband.

"I'll be there soon," he replies. "Only 1:58 left on the clock."

He's watching another classic Duke-North Carolina college basketball matchup on TV. It's a close battle at Cameron Indoor Stadium, and the clock is winding down.

But can the Mrs. expect the Mr. to actually be done watching the game in less than 2 minutes? The truth is, each team will use the two full time-outs and the 20-second time-out if they have it left. Both are in the double bonus. Free throws will be flying. The TV people have their commercials to air. The game will eventually go into double overtime, and it will be more than an hour before the husband gets to bed. In the upside-down math of a basketball game-clock, sometimes 2 minutes equals 1 hour.

FAST FACT:
In 1990 NCAA basketball teams began using clocks calibrated to tenths of a second.

There's evidence throughout the Bible that God's game-clock is a little like that. It doesn't always run on the same time we do. For example, "By faith Joseph, when his end was near, spoke about the exodus of the Israelites from Egypt and gave instructions about his bones"(Hebrews 11:22). Joseph believed that God would make good on His promise to give Israel the Promised Land—so much so that he wanted to make sure that after he died, his bones would be carried back to Palestine and buried there. But do you think he had any idea that the Israelites would be in Egypt for 400 years? Or that they would spend 40 years in the wilderness before entering the Land?

Do you sometimes wonder if God will provide for you as He promised? Those who live by faith must live by faith in God's time. God's game-clock will read :00 right when it should. —BRIAN HETTINGA

FOLLOW THROUGH

Name a situation in which you are waiting for God to provide (health, relationship, children, etc.). Would you expect that waiting would be part of our lives as we live by faith?

From the Playbook: Look at the people of faith mentioned in Hebrews 11:8–22—Abraham, Isaac, Jacob, and Joseph—and note how often they had to wait for God to fulfill His promises to them.

TOP 25 GREAT BASKETBALL GAMES

SIX OVERTIMES! **March 12, 2009, Syracuse 127, Connecticut 117**—That was the score. But other numbers tell the story. Six overtimes. In those extra sessions, 102 points were scored. The score at the end of regulation was 71-71. Eight players fouled out. The teams shot 103 times in the overtime sessions. The teams played 70 minutes of basketball. Combined, the teams shot 48 free throws in overtime. In the first five overtimes, Syracuse was never ahead. The game took three hours and 46 minutes to play.

50. BE AN EXAMPLE

Game Plan:
Showing the way for others

"Don't let anyone look down on you because you are young, but set an example." 1 TIMOTHY 4:12

On the court for one high school basketball team was a talented group of African-American players. The other team consisted of an equally talented group of white players. One ref was white. One was black. On one side of the court sat the African-American fans; on the other side, the white.

FAST FACT:

Grant Hill won the NBA Sportsmanship Award trophy three times during his career.

As the two teams battled each other, tensions were high—for the teams were battling for a regional championship. Neither team could muster much of a lead, and every call by the refs was met with disdain by the fans of one of the teams. Occasionally, it appeared that fans on either side might break out of control.

Yet on the court, the players never strayed from their focus on hard play and good sportsmanship. Despite the fouls, the occasional bump, and the nonstop action, they never lost control of their poise.

As the game ended, the two teams congratulated each other in a show of good sportsmanship.

These teenage boys had shown supreme maturity, clearheadedness, and class—while their moms and dads were about to come apart in the stands all around them.

This show of maturity can teach us a lot about the difference young people can make in our world. There are adults out there who need to see the example set by teens who have self-control and discipline. All around are adults who think it's okay to lie, steal, cheat, commit adultery, and get involved in all kinds of destructive behavior.

Are you a teen? Stand above all that. "Set an example," Paul said. Be a model for all who look at you. Live right. Honor God with your life. Show the way for the older people in your life. —DAVE BRANON

FOLLOW THROUGH

When have you made mistakes by expecting less of yourself than you should have? Can you somehow salvage that situation? Be a model for the older generation.

From the Playbook: Read Daniel 1.

TOP 25 GREAT BASKETBALL GAMES

TEXAS WESTERN BREAKS THROUGH   March 19, 1966, Texas Western Miners 72, Kentucky Wildcats 65—Even without the historical importance of this game, it would have had plenty of built-in drama. For instance, Kentucky was a college basketball powerhouse, and Texas Western was an unknown on the major college hoops scene. But Don Haskins had overcome prejudices and stereotypes to put together a remarkable basketball team. The fact that the top five players on his team were African-Americans would be unimportant these days, but in 1966, it was a groundbreaking achievement. Led by Bobby Joe Hill, David Lattin, and Nevil Shed, Texas Western beat Adolph Rupp's squad 72-65 to change the face of NCAA hoops forever.

51. THE LEGACY OF ERNIE HARWELL

Game Plan:
Learning from our elders

"Gray hair is a crown of splendor; it is attained by a righteous life." PROVERBS 16:31

Few sports figures of the twentieth century set forth a life of honor and respect as did legendary baseball announcer Ernie Harwell.

Each year, from those first melodious words of spring when he introduced the baseball season with words from the Song of Solomon until his final farewell at the end of the year, Mr. Harwell provided a soothing yet exciting verbal picture of baseball for fans across the Midwest.

Everyone who ever met Ernie says that although he was one of the greatest play-by-play announcers ever, he was a better person than he was an announcer.

That's because there was more than just baseball in Ernie's heart. There was also a kindness and a joy of living that came directly from his personal relationship with Jesus Christ. He lived out his faith without being obtrusive, plus he demonstrated the value of his faith when adversity crossed his path.

One of those times was in the 1990s when his employer, the Detroit Tigers, inexplicably fired him. While fans responded in anger and

FAST FACT:
When Ernie Harwell was a boy growing up in Atlanta, he delivered newspapers. One of the customers on his route was Margaret Mitchell, who wrote Gone With the Wind. *Ernie's brother, Richard, a Civil War historian and writer, owned the first signed copy of* Gone With the Wind.

disgust, Ernie continued to carry himself with a dignity and self-effacing humor. He said simply, "God blessed me by putting me here for 31 years." When later the Tigers re-instated Harwell to his rightful place in the radio booth, not a single bitter word came from his lips.

How much we can learn from the classy way Ernie Harwell lived his life. He even handled the news of the cancer that would claim his life with godly faith, calling it another great adventure. Imagine how different this world would be if we all as fellow Christians would leave an Ernie-Harwell type legacy.

Thanks, Ernie, for showing the way.   —DAVE BRANON

FOLLOW THROUGH

If someone were to write an article about your life so far, how do you think you would be described? Would "God-honoring" come to mind?

From the Playbook: Read Proverbs15:16–24.

TOP 25 GREAT BASEBALL GAMES

THE SHOT HEARD AROUND THE (BASEBALL) WORLD October 3, 1951, New York Giants 5, Brooklyn Dodgers 4—The New York Giants trailed 4-1 going into the bottom of the ninth in the deciding game of a 3-game NL playoff to see who would win the pennant and play in the World Series. When Don Newcombe allowed a run to score and had runners at first and third, Brooklyn manager Charlie Dressen pulled starter Newcombe and brought in Ralph Branca. Although Branca had already given up a home run in the series to Bobby Thomson, he was called on again. Thomson hit Branca's second pitch over the left-field seats for a 5-4 win in one of the most dramatic finishes in baseball history. Ernie Harwell was in the broadcast booth that day doing the game for television.

52. TAKE ME OUT TO THE BALL GAME

Game Plan:
Checking up on our motives

"[The Lord] will ... expose the motives of men's hearts."
1 CORINTHIANS 4:5

Each year when baseball season rolls around again, I find myself pondering a deep question: Why during the seventh inning stretch do we sing the song "Take Me Out to the Ball Game" if we are already at the game?

Okay. I'll admit that's not really a deep question. In fact, it's silly. What I'm asking about is rather off the wall. But the process of asking why—well, that's not strange in and of itself.

Motives—the reasons we do what we do—are not irrelevant. They are important. Jesus said to the religious leaders of His day, "These people honor me with their lips, but their hearts are far from me" (Matthew 15:8). It all comes down to motive.

For instance, I can say to an athlete, "You played an awesome game." On the surface this looks like a good thing to say, but my motive for saying it could be selfish. Rather than building someone up, I could really be trying to impress others with my "encouragement." I could be looking for some kind of favor from the guy.

The book of Proverbs says, "All a man's ways seem innocent to him, but motives are weighed by the Lord" (Proverbs 16:2).

We should never obsess about motives, but it is important to be aware that we might not be as innocent as we think we are.

It's good to ask ourselves why we do what we do. Questioning our motives can give us a snapshot of the condition of our heart. It's the heart that counts to God, so what we do should be done for God's glory—not ours. Now, that's a fantastic motive.

—JEFF OLSON

FOLLOW THROUGH

Be open to the fact that your motives for doing some things are not as innocent as you think. Then decide how to make the needed change in motives.

From the Playbook: Read Proverbs 16:1–7.

TOP 25 GREAT BASEBALL GAMES

BELIEVE IT, JACK **October 15, 1988, Los Angeles Dodgers 5, Oakland A's 4**—Fans watching at home had already been told not to expect anything from Kirk Gibson. His knee hurt too much. But Tommy Lasorda needed instant offense, so Gibson limped to home plate with the Dodgers trailing 4-3 in the bottom of the ninth. One runner was on base for LA. Gibson stood in against Dennis Eckersley and hit one of the most iconic home runs in major league history, lifting the LA Dodgers to a victory over the Oakland A's. It was Gibson's only at-bat of the World Series, but it was enough to boost the Dodgers to a world championship. When he hit it, announcer Jack Buck proclaimed, "I don't believe what I just saw." He was not alone.

53. ARE YOU OPTIMISTIC?

Game Plan:
Looking ahead with hope

"Having the hope of eternal life." Titus 3:7

At the start of every major league baseball season, all 30 teams are optimistic. For some, the expectations include a World Series run. For others, the dream would be a trip to the playoffs, but the reality is the hope of a .500 season. For most big league clubs, there are many "ifs" in the new season equation. If young players develop quickly, if veterans stay healthy, if everybody hits.

For instance, it seems that each season the New York Yankees expect to win—or at least be in contention for—another World Series crown. Conversely, a team like the Pittsburgh Pirates would love to battle through a tough National League season and finish with a .500 season.

FAST FACT:
No wonder the New York Yankees are optimistic: They have won one-fourth of all World Series since the early 1900s.

For followers of Jesus Christ, we don't have to settle for a .500 or better view when considering our future. We don't have to struggle with loss after loss with no hope for the future. The apostle Paul reveals the reason for our optimism in his letter to Titus.

The apostle shows us that in the midst of our sinful lives, in the midst of our rebellion against God—Jesus came. God poured out his grace and mercy upon those who believe in Jesus.

Therefore, because of this grace—you and I should not be pessimistic. Jesus has made us "heirs having the hope of eternal life" (Titus 3:7).

No matter how bleak the season of life we are facing looks

to us today, you and I can be genuinely optimistic. We have hope through the grace of Jesus! —ROB BENTZ

FOLLOW THROUGH

Pray to God and thank Him that you are justified by His grace and therefore have the hope of eternal life. If you do not have this hope, place your faith in Christ. The words of the following prayer can guide you: *God, I confess that I am a sinner in need of forgiveness. I repent of my sin and place my faith in Jesus Christ, who lived a holy life and gave that life as a payment for my sin. Thank you for making me an heir of eternal life. Amen.*

From the Playbook: Read and meditate on Titus 3:3–8.

TOP 25 GREAT BASEBALL GAMES

THE PERFECT GAME **September 9, 1965, Los Angeles Dodgers 1, Chicago Cubs 0**—Like no other game in baseball history, this game between the LA Dodgers and the Chicago Cubs flirted with absolute mound perfection. Most notably, Sandy Koufax pitched his first perfect game—his fourth no-hitter—and he struck out 14 batters. But his opponent, Bob Hendley, was nearly as good. Both had no-hitters going into the seventh inning—Hendley ended with a one-hitter, and the run that did score was unearned. Only two batters reached base in the game, marking the only time in major league history that has happened. The absolute minimum, of course, is one.

54. WHAT WILL THE OUTCOME BE?

"Blessed are the meek, for they will inherit the earth."
MATTHEW 5:5

Although baseball's National League Giants won several league championships in the past few decades, they went 55 years—between 1954 and 2009—before winning the World Series in 2010. A popular myth explaining the Giants' 50-plus-year failure to win the Fall Classic was called the "Krukow Kurse."

Here's how the story goes: Before the start of each baseball season, former big league pitcher Mike Krukow, a broadcaster for the Giants, would optimistically predict on his radio show that, "This is the season the Giants will win it all!" Krukow, however, has been wrong every year, prompting many people believe that once Krukow stops predicting the Giants will win, they will in fact win. Of course, the 2010 championship has ended the so-called curse.

FAST FACT:
The Giants were World Series champions five times between 1905 and 1954.

Making a prediction means "to tell about something in advance of its occurrence by means of special knowledge or inference." But just as meteorologists are sometimes wrong with their weather forecasts, so are the rest of us rarely able to predict with 100-percent accuracy the outcome of future events.

The only outcomes we can count on with certainty are those that God's Word says will happen. For example, in Matthew 5:5, we are promised that God will bless His children who are humble in spirit. The New Testament verse says, "Blessed are the meek, for they will inherit the earth." God doesn't say the meek might inherit the kingdom of God. He says they absolutely will.

Think about how your goals might change if they were based on God's Word—and if you were to live according to God's promises instead of the world's predictions.

—ROXANNE ROBBINS

FOLLOW THROUGH

Ask a Christian mentor to help you locate some of God's promises (or prophecies) in the Old Testament that have already come true as God promised they would.

From the Playbook: Read Matthew 5.

TOP 25 GREAT BASEBALL GAMES

FISK'S BODY ENGLISH   October 21, 1975, Boston Red Sox 7, Cincinnati Reds 6—The Boston Red Sox hadn't won a World Series in 57 years, and they were facing the indomitable Big Red Machine, which had won the NL West by 20 games and had swept Pittsburgh in the NLCS. Cincy had taken a 3-2 Series lead. After both teams sat out three days of rain in Boston, play resumed for Game 6. The Sox took an early 3-0 lead on a Fred Lynn home run. In the fifth, the Reds tied the game at 3-3. By the time the Sox came to bat in the eighth, Cincinnati was up 6-3 and was just six outs from a WS title. Former Reds outfielder Bernie Carbo tied things in the eighth with a three-run shot. The teams battled scorelessly into the 12th, when Carlton Fisk hit a long drive down the leftfield line. He waved vigorously at the ball and it magically stayed fair—hitting the foul pole for a game-winning home run.

55. MY AWFUL WEEK

Game Plan:
Turning your failures into successes

*"Though a righteous man falls seven times,
he rises again."* PROVERBS 24:16

My senior year of high school baseball was memorable. Good pitching and solid defense helped us sweep a doubleheader against the defending state champs. Now ranked No. 9 in the state, we were flying high.

And then ... Down 2-1, tying run on second, two outs, last inning. I'm batting. Two strikes. Then two balls. Then two fouls straight back. Then a swing and a miss.

FAST FACT:

Fred Merkle, just 19 years old, made a base-running blunder in 1908 for the New York Giants that let the Chicago Cubs get to the World Series—where they won their last World Series championship!

Fast-forward two days. Last inning of a 1-1 tie, our opponent has the winning run on second. I cheat in from left field. Line drive over the glove of the shortstop. I race to my right, reach down, and come up for the throw—without the ball. It lies forlornly behind me, reachable, but much too late to save the game.

I single-handedly knocked us out of the Top 10. But I learned some valuable life lessons that difficult week. My coach put me right back in the lineup. I learned about resilience and mental toughness. And I'm stronger for it.

During the worst—and greatest—week in human history, Simon Peter denied his Lord three times (Matthew 26:69–75). Hours later, Jesus was crucified on a cross.

Peter, we might decide, was a failure. He had let Jesus down during His time of trouble—despite having promised to die for Him if he had to.

Fast-forward a few weeks. Peter stood by the Sea of Galilee with Jesus and some of the disciples. Three times Jesus asked him, "Simon son of John, do you love me?" And Jesus restored Peter, giving him the incomparable task of feeding Jesus' "sheep" (John 21:15–17). Peter became one of the most successful preachers ever, and history has never been the same.

Think you're failing? Turn to Jesus. He takes our biggest failures and turns them into something good.

—TIM GUSTAFSON

FOLLOW THROUGH

What are some of the difficult things that have happened to you, on or off the playing field? How can adversity in sports help you handle adversity in life? How does Jesus want us to handle adversity?

From the Playbook: Read Matthew 26:69–75, John 21:15–17.

TOP 25 GREAT BASEBALL GAMES

MAGIC MAZ **October 1960, Pittsburgh Pirates 10, New York Yankees 9**—Some think Bill Mazeroski is in the Baseball Hall of Fame because of one swing of the bat. And what a swing it was! Game 7 of the Series against the Yankees. Bobby Richardson had killed Pirates' pitching, racking up 12 RBI. But as the Pirates batted in the bottom of the ninth, the score was tied at 9-9. Ralph Terry was the Yankees' pitcher. The first pitch was a ball, but the second was in Mazeroski's zone. He hit it over the left-field fence in Forbes Field for the first walk-off home run in World Series history. Maz, who hit just .260 in his 17 seasons, was inducted into the Hall of Fame in 2001.

56. AS IF IT NEVER HAPPENED

Game Plan:
Reveling in the joy of God's forgiveness

"If we walk in the light, as he is in the light, we have fellowship with one another, and the blood of Jesus, his Son, purifies us from all sin." 1 JOHN 1:7

It was a typically breezy April day in the Windy City. Yet what took place at the Friendly Confines was anything but typical.

Pitching for the Chicago Cubs on that day was Kerry Wood; his counterpart for the San Diego Padres was a hard-thrower named Adam Eaton. What's so significant about this match-up? Both hurlers had four-inch scars down the side of their pitching elbows. Both pitchers had experienced the operation known as Tommy John surgery (a surgical procedure in which doctors remove a ligament from the pitcher's wrist or hamstring and graft it into the elbow. Technically, it's known as ulnar collateral ligament reconstruction).

FAST FACT:
Tommy John had the experimental surgery that was named after him in 1974. Dr. Frank Jobe did the surgery.

Following the game, Wood told reporters he was actually "throwing harder consistently" following the surgery. Another pitcher who experienced Tommy John surgery was former Cy Young winner Pat Hentgen. The former Blue Jays ace, who retired from baseball in 2004, said about the results of the surgery, "as far as the way my arm feels, it feels like it never happened."

This sort of new physical beginning can help us think of the new spiritual beginning we receive when we repent of our sin and receive the grace that is ours through personal faith in Jesus Christ. The sacrificial blood of Jesus Christ on the cross purifies those who have turned to Him seeking forgiveness. He makes us new.

The broken body and shed blood of Jesus on the cross gives forgiveness and freedom from the penalty of sin that you and I deserve. Jesus washes us clean. He cleanses our sin with His righteousness. When you and I stand before the Father on judgment day, God will consider our sins as though they never happened—thanks to the amazing sacrifice of Jesus.   —ROB BENTZ

FOLLOW THROUGH

Have you repented of your sin and placed your faith in Jesus Christ? If not, I encourage you to pray the following prayer of repentance and faith. *"God, I confess that I am a sinner in need of forgiveness. I repent of my sin and place my faith in Jesus Christ, who lived a holy life and gave that life as a payment for my sin. Thank you for making me clean because of Jesus. Amen."*

From the Playbook: Read John 1:5–10.

TOP 25
GREAT BASEBALL GAMES

MARATHON AT MINUTE MAID   **October 9, 2005, Houston 7, Atlanta 6**—Quick. Name all the Chris Burke highlights you can think of. If indeed Burke had others besides this game, none came close to matching the drama. But first, there were enough baseball highlights to keep *SportsCenter* busy all night. The Braves scored early and often, taking a 6-1 lead into the eighth inning. The stunned Minute Maid crowd in Houston could see World Series dreams fading away. But in the eighth, Lance Berkman blasted a grand slam to make it 6-5. And in the bottom of the ninth, Brad Ausmus hit a two-out home run to send the game into extra innings. Roger Clemens came in as a relief pitcher in the fifteenth inning, and he held the Braves scoreless until Burke ended it and sent the Astros to the NLCS against St. Louis with his game-winning home run in the eighteenth inning.

57. MOSES, HOPE, AND THE CHICAGO CUBS

Game Plan:
Depending on God's will

"Now faith is being sure of what we hope for and certain of what we do not see." HEBREWS 11:1

Season after season, fans of the Chicago Cubs end up saying the same thing. "Wait 'til next year."

It's quite optimistic to be sure, especially since next year inevitably ends up looking like the year before. Hope springs eternal each spring training as fans believe that somehow, some way, the Cubs will reach the World Series.

FAST FACT:

The last time the Chicago Cubs won the World Series (unless they do so after this book goes to press), the US had 88 million citizens, Teddy Roosevelt was president, and a new Ford cost $850.

In 2003, the Cubs led the Florida Marlins three games to one in the National League Championship Series and were five outs away from reaching the World Series when things again fell apart. In 2008, the Cubs won 97 games during the season but lost in the Division Series in three games to the Dodgers. For more than a century—since 1908—the Cubs did not win the World Series.

Pretty sad, huh?

Yet, fans continue to hope.

Read Hebrews 11 and check out all the mentions of people who have depended on faith to carry them through their lives. Faith, verse one tells us, requires us to put our trust in things we don't yet see. That's tough, for sure, especially since we usually like to have evidence that something will happen. But faith requires us to put ourselves out there.

Throughout Hebrews 11, we are reminded that people like

Noah, Abraham and Moses—three of the Bible's big hitters—were asked to do things that, at the time, didn't make sense. Yet each trusted God, hoping that He would be true to His word and deliver what He had promised.

We all struggle sometimes with putting our complete hope in the Lord—especially when He asks us to do something that we don't at first understand. But if, as did his three servants and scores of others throughout the Bible, we have the faith to believe God will be faithful, we know this: Things will work out according to His will.

That's so much better than saying, "Wait 'til next year."

—JEFF ARNOLD

FOLLOW THROUGH

Discover one area of your life that you have difficulty turning over to God. You have seen Him handle other concerns in your life, and He's promised He won't give you more than you can handle. What's stopping you from handing everything over to Him? Jesus won't let you down.

From the Playbook: Read Hebrews 11.

GREAT BASEBALL GAMES

WORLD SERIES PERFECTION October 8, 1956, New York Yankees 2, Brooklyn Dodgers 0—New York Yankees pitcher Don Larsen sure knew how to pick his spots. He never won more than 11 games in a season. In fact, he lost 21 games in 1954. But on October 8, 1956, at Yankee Stadium against the Brooklyn Dodgers, he put it all together. With a little help from Mickey Mantle, who made a sensational catch of a Gil Hodges drive and who hit a home run to provide half the offense Larsen needed, the 27-year-old pitcher threw the only perfect game in World Series history.

58. TAKE TIME TO REST

Game Plan:
Schedule break times in life

*"Six days you shall labor, but on the seventh day
you shall rest."* EXODUS 34:21

Professional athletes who hope to keep playing at the highest level understand the value of the offseason. It's during those weeks or months, when they're less prone to be in the public eye and when they're not under the pressure of league competition, that athletes must work hard to rest while also laying the foundation for peak performance when the new season comes around.

Mike Sweeney, whose successful major-league career included being named to the American League All-Star team five times, demonstrated this during one offseason. That winter, he followed an intense regimen developed by one of the Kansas City Royals' former strength and conditioning coaches. Sweeney's goal was to heal neck and back injuries that slowed him the previous few seasons as he played for the Royals.

An offseason for a professional athlete might be comparable to a student's summer off from school or an employee's vacation from a job. Regardless of what it is we're getting time off from, it's up to us how we're going to spend that break. We can be lazy and return in poor shape, or we can strive to balance relaxation with activities and habits that will make us even sharper when we return.

I have a friend who owns a little store. She often has mini "offseasons" between customers and spends that time reading her Bible. I asked her recently about her Bible reading, and she replied, "It's often very slow here [at the store], and so I read my Bible. God gives me the time to read."

Where in your schedule is God giving you the time to rest, read His Word, and get yourself rested, retooled, and revitalized for the next section of life? During your little "offseasons," are you getting ready for the action ahead?

—ROXANNE ROBBINS

FOLLOW THROUGH

Write down three goals that will help you use times of rest to grow closer to the Lord.

From the Playbook: Read Exodus 34:20–22.

TOP 25 GREAT BASEBALL GAMES

JUMPIN' JOE CARTER   October 23, 1993, Toronto Blue Jays 8, Philadelphia Phillies 6—Joe Carter's dramatic ending to the 1993 World Series had to have lots of drama and excitement—it would have to last two whole seasons. When Carter smacked a Mitch Williams pitch over the left-field fence to end the 1993 Fall Classic and give the Toronto Blue Jays the championship, it would be the last World Series at-bat until 1995. The Series was cancelled in 1994 for a so-called work stoppage. Carter's jubilant, triumphant, jump-filled trip around the bases was a fitting end to a string of 90-plus consecutive years of World Series for major league baseball.

59. WHAT BIG MAC LACKS

Game Plan:
Living by God's commands

"Asa did what was right in the eyes of the Lord."
1 KINGS 15:11

His numbers are legendary. He swatted 583 home runs and had a slugging percentage of .588 (both Top 10 numbers of all-time). But when Mark McGwire was up for election to the Baseball Hall of Fame for the first time in 2007, just 23.5 percent of the ballots cast gave him the nod.

So what happened? Baseball writers believed then and now know that Big Mac used steroids to bash baseballs over outfield fences. The man who once hit 70 home runs in one MLB season may never be elected to the Hall of Fame because of his use of performance-enhancing drugs.

FAST FACT:
In 2007, McGwire finished behind Gwynn, Ripken, Rich Gossage, Jim Rice, Andre Dawson, Bert Blyleven, Lee Smith, and Jack Morris in HOF voting.

Big Mac had an amazing 16-year career in the Show, but he may live his remaining years without the satisfaction of making it to baseball's biggest house. His reputation has eclipsed his accomplishments. In the same summer that 2007 inductees Tony Gwynn and Cal Ripken Jr. were basking in the bright lights and loving embraces of their induction into the Hall of Fame in Cooperstown, Mark McGwire was left out in the cold.

It's obvious that lacking a good reputation can be a bitter thing. To contrast this statement, we meet a king in the Old Testament who had a great reputation! What's more impressive, Asa was the first king in Judah to have a great rep, and his name is forever positively recorded in the Bible.

What did he do to earn this acclaim? Two things stand out:

1. He "did what was right in the eyes of the Lord" (1 Kings 15:11); 2. His "heart was fully committed to the Lord all his life" (v. 14).

Did you catch that? A life well lived requires the correct focus: following God's commands and consistency—living that way 24/7. A good rep will naturally follow!

—Tom Felten

FOLLOW THROUGH

Make a list of five people you feel have a great reputation. What's different about them? What are characteristics that highlight their way of living? What will you do today to live in an Asa-like way that honors God?

From the Playbook: Read 1 Kings 15:8–24.

TOP 25 GREAT BASEBALL GAMES

SMOLTZ FACES HIS HERO **October 27, 1991, Minnesota Twins 1, Atlanta Braves 0**—This was the "tomorrow night" in Jack Buck's memorable "We'll see you tomorrow night" call of Kirby Puckett's game-winning home run in Game 6. Playing in the Metrodome, the Minnesota Twins and the Atlanta Braves—both worst-to-first teams from 1990 to 1991—sent their aces to the mound. John Smoltz, a Michigan native who followed former Tiger pitcher Jack Morris as a kid, faced his hero in the concluding game of what some call the best World Series ever. The two superstar pitchers didn't disappoint. The game was scoreless going into the eighth inning. The Braves got a single and a double but didn't score. The Twins had runners at first and third with one out in the bottom of the inning but didn't score. Morris pitched on. He retired the Braves in order in the tenth, and finally the Twins scored a run to win the game 1-0 and take the Series.

60. EXTRA BOOST?

*"You were bought at a price. Therefore, honor God
with your body."* 1 Corinthians 6:20

Is it right or wrong for an athlete to take performance-enhancing supplements to enhance his or her ability in sports? The answer might depend on your answer to another question.

Does the Lord live inside of you?

If you answered yes, is it purely "figurative," a mere expression made to reflect His closeness? Or is it literally true? How you believe about that will affect how you live.

FAST FACT:

Two-time World Series champ Chad Curtis, who is not a big guy at 5-10, 175, challenges kids by reminding them, "I got to the highest level of pro sports without drugs."

The Bible says, "Do you not know that your body is a temple of the Holy Spirit, who is in you, whom you have received from God? You are not your own; you were bought at a price. Therefore honor God with your body" (1 Corinthians 6:19-20).

Catcher Chad Moeller, while playing for the Milwaukee Brewers, commented on the supplements issue in the context of the overall relationship between the physical, spiritual, emotional, and mental aspects of life.

"The body is a temple for the Lord," said Moeller, who hit for the cycle in a game in 2004 (single, double, triple, and home run). "We're blessed to have it, blessed we're able to walk around on this planet and do the things we do. We have to treat ourselves like we'd want to treat the Lord.

"I have to keep my body in shape, in peak performance, as finely tuned as possible because it's where the Lord spends His time, inside of me and you. If He's going to use me that way, and if I'm not taking care of myself, He's not going to have a forum to spread himself. And if I abuse myself, I'm abusing Him."

There's your answer. If you are a Christian, the Holy Spirit is the only "extra boost" you need. —VICTOR LEE

FOLLOW THROUGH

What else does it mean that your body is the temple of the Holy Spirit? Taken seriously, this teaching would change some things in your life, including what three aspects?

From the Playbook: Read 1 Corinthians 6:12–20.

TOP 25 GREAT BASEBALL GAMES

FIREWORKS, FINALLY July 4–5, 1985, New York Mets 16, Atlanta Braves 11—It was the Fourth of July in Atlanta, and fireworks were on the docket. But then it rained and the game was delayed 90 minutes. And then it rained again in the third inning, so this time 41 more minutes ticked away. Meanwhile, both the Braves and the New York Mets were scoring early and often. At the end of eight innings, the score was 8-8. Both teams scored twice in the ninth, so the game went into extra innings. The fireworks would have to wait. The teams toiled through eight more innings until the Mets scored to take an 11-10 lead. In the bottom of the 18th, the Braves had run out of players to pinch-hit, so pitcher Rick Camp, a .074 career hitter had to bat with two outs and the game on the line. Of course, he hit a home run to send the game into the 19th. Though the fireworks stayed unlit, the Mets exploded for five runs, and the Braves could muster just two runs, and the game finally ended. Fourth of July fireworks became a Fifth of July celebration—at 4:01 a.m.

61. DON'T IMITATE HIM

Game Plan:
Patterning our lives after the right Person

"Dear friend, do not imitate what is evil, but what is good." 3 JOHN 11

As a Little League baseball player, I loved to imitate all of my favorite players and pattern my game after theirs. Growing up in Michigan, I followed the Detroit Tigers. Their powerhouse teams of the 80s featured sluggers Lance Parrish and Kirk Gibson, as well as slick infielders Lou Whitaker and Alan Trammell. All were great players with sound fundamental skills that were available for an impressionable little leaguer to copy.

FAST FACT:
John Wockenfuss played in the big leagues for 12 seasons with the Tigers and the Philadelphia Phillies. He finished with a .262 career batting average.

But there was one Detroit Tiger my Little League coach—my dad—never wanted me to imitate. His name was John B. Wockenfuss.

Wockenfuss, a back-up catcher for the Tigers in the early 80s, had one of the most unconventional methods of batting of any major league player before or since. "Johnny B" used a dramatically closed stance. But that wasn't the weird part—he used to wave his top hand at the pitcher while in the batter's box.

Wockenfuss was the last person a coach would want his players watching for batting tips. His fundamentals were, to the Little League coach, simply wrong.

As Christians, there are plenty of behaviors that strike against the fundamentals of our faith. There are plenty of thoughts and actions that are evil! In 3 John 11, believers are exhorted to imitate what is good—not what is evil. And in

1 Corinthians 11:1, Paul says that we should imitate him—but only as he follows the righteous example of Christ.

Are you finding it easier in your life to imitate the evil things? Are you battling peer pressure to give in and emulate the evil desires of your friends/teammates/students/co-workers?

God doesn't require perfect actions and/or behavior. But He does desire that we pattern our lives after His Son, Jesus, and those who imitate Him. For the believer, that's the right person to follow.

—ROB BENTZ

FOLLOW THROUGH

Who are you patterning your life after? If it's not your Savior Jesus, ask God in prayer to give you a passion to be more Christlike.

From the Playbook: Read 3 John.

TOP 25
GREAT BASEBALL GAMES

PHILLY LEAVES A MESSAGE **October 1, 1950, Philadelphia Phillies 4, Brooklyn Dodgers 1**—Two days after the telephone answering machine was invented in New Jersey, the Philadelphia Phillies relayed a word to the Brooklyn Dodgers: We're No. 1. Heading into this final contest of the 1950 regular season at Ebbets Field in Brooklyn, Philly held a one-game lead in the National League. With the score tied 1-1 in the ninth, the Phillies' Richie Ashburn threw out Cal Abrams at the plate to stop the Dodgers from scoring the winning run. Then, in the 10th, Dick Sisler hit a three-run home run to give the Phillies the game and the National League pennant.

62. A LEGACY OF RESILIENCE

Game Plan:
Facing adversity with God's help

"Daniel resolved not to defile himself." DANIEL 1:8

As a youth soccer coach, I'm learning a lot about human nature. Some kids quit easily; others turn setbacks into gains. Some kids think a loss is the end of the world. Others forget about it quickly or find moral victories. All kids who play soccer eat a lot! And often.

I doubt that Mickey Lolich ever played soccer, but he did eat a lot. But much more important to our discussion, he turned a childhood setback (and what kid who plays youth soccer, baseball, or basketball doesn't have those) into something great.

FAST FACT:

Tim Gustafson, former editor of Our Daily Bread, *will have plenty of opportunities to coach kids' sports. He and his wife Leisa have eight children—seven of them boys.*

As a kid, Mickey injured his right arm, which is bad if you're an aspiring pitcher. So the natural right-hander decided he would turn around and pitch left-handed. With hard work, he transformed himself into a major league pitcher—as a lefty! He even pitched three complete-game victories in the 1968 World Series for the Detroit Tigers. Never mind your off-arm; try doing that with your dominant arm!

The prophet Daniel overcame adversity much worse than a broken arm or a soccer loss. Torn from his homeland by a murderous regime, he was, some scholars believe, made a eunuch by his captors. Ordered to do things that would violate his moral conscience, he courageously stood up to godless enemies who sought his death—showing us all the meaning of genuine manhood. Daniel eventually rose to third in command in the most powerful kingdom of the day (Daniel 5:29). And he did it without compromising his faith.

How did one man accomplish so much? By a resilient and persistent faith in God, despite all the terrible things that had happened to him.

Whatever adversity you face today, there's no telling what God can do with it if you are willing to trust His plan for your life. —Tim Gustafson

FOLLOW THROUGH

What adversity faces you today? How are you reacting to it? How can the Holy Spirit help you react appropriately?

From the Playbook: Read Daniel 6:13–22.

TOP 25 GREAT BASEBALL GAMES

DRAMA IN THE DOME   **October 15, 1986, New York Mets 7, Houston Astros 6**—Battling to win the NL pennant, the Astros and Mets had already played five tough, tight games in the NLCS—three of which were decided by one run. This time, it was hard to get even that one-run differential. The Astros led 3-0 at the Astrodome until the Mets tied the game in the top of the ninth. In the 14th both teams scored to keep the game going. In the 16th, NY scored three and the Astros could only muster two, so the visitors won the series 4-2 and went on to the World Series.

63. THE COMPLAIN GAME

Game Plan:
Leaving matters in God's hands

"Do everything without complaining or arguing."
PHILIPPIANS 2:14

It happens without fail. It's the bottom of the ninth inning, there are two outs, and the tying run is dancing off second base. The batter smacks a line drive to center field, and the fielder scoops up the ball and fires it to the catcher on one hop. The runner slides across the plate, appearing to beat the throw home.

But the umpire jabs his thumb into the air to signal that the runner is out, and the offended manager comes storming out of the dugout to protest.

The TV instant replay shows the runner is clearly safe, and the manager knows it as well. He gets into the umpire's face, yelling and screaming. And what happens? He gets his way, right?

Sorry, but no.

Life, like baseball, does not always go our way.

Some days even when it appears that circumstances will turn out as we want them to—something happens to change it. How do we handle it when the call—or the day—doesn't go our way?

In Philippians 2, we are instructed to do everything without complaining so that we may be found blameless and pure before God. Granted, that's not easy to do. It's easier to be like that manager and yell and scream and tell God that what is happening to us isn't fair. But just as in that ninth-inning situation, does our arguing change things?

Usually not. Remember, God is in control—not us. And He knows far better than we do what is best for us. If our goal is to be blameless, complaining won't get us very far toward reaching that goal. In fact, complaining will set us back in our efforts to be godly.

When things don't go our way, remember this: God has the better view of our lives. We need to trust Him. And not complain.

—JEFF ARNOLD

FOLLOW THROUGH

Why not make an effort today to get through the day without complaining or arguing. It's tough, but just think—the way you handle something you don't like is a direct reflection on your testimony for Jesus.

From the Playbook: Read Philippians 2.

TOP 25 GREAT BASEBALL GAMES

DENT DINGS THE RED SOX **October 2, 1978, New York Yankees 5, Boston Red Sox 4**—After blowing a 14-game lead and falling 3 games behind the Yankees, the Red Sox roared back to tie the Yanks and force a one-game showdown for the right to advance to the playoffs. In the seventh inning, infielder Bucky Dent, who would hit just 40 home runs in 12 years of major-league play, smacked a 3-run homer that glanced off the top of the Green Monster to put the Yanks on top. They won the game 5-4 to extend the Curse of the Bambino one more year.

64. IN A SLUMP?

Game Plan:
Overcoming tough times

"Why are you downcast, O my soul? Why so disturbed within me?" PSALM 42:5

To call Brad Lidge's 2006 season a slump would be an understatement. The closer for the Houston Astros got roughed up on a regular basis. Check out his numbers: 5.28 ERA, 36 walks in 75 innings, 10 home runs—including a pair of grand slams, and six blown saves. Not exactly "lights out" as the scoreboard in Houston often read when Lidge was on the hill for the 'Stros.

The man who dominated batters in 2005 (2.28 ERA and 42 saves) had a difficult time simply getting outs in 2006. And then in 2008, Lidge was again among the best in the game, going the whole season without blowing a save.

FAST FACT:

Brad Lidge won the Rolaids Relief Man of the Year Award in 2008. He had 41 saves and an ERA of 1.95.

Our lives go through ups and downs just like that of a big-league closer. Obviously, we are not under the same public spotlight and scrutiny, yet we often deal with difficulties that leave us bewildered and frustrated.

We often read in the Bible about people's highs and lows. Perhaps nowhere in the Scriptures do we see good times and rough times described so succinctly as we do in the Psalms.

The psalmist battled through difficult times. He questioned God. He asked questions about God's involvement in his daily life. He wondered openly about where God was when he needed Him the most.

Yet in the midst of his real-life struggle and doubt, the

psalmist had a firm foundation (faith to trust in God in all things). That's why we see a measure of hope in his writings in Psalm 42. In spite of his current circumstances and feelings, he remained hopeful. "Why are you downcast, O my soul? Why so disturbed within me? Put your hope in God, for I will yet praise him, my Savior and my God" (Psalm 42:11).

Because of God's faithfulness, we can trust Him in good times and bad.   —ROB BENTZ

FOLLOW THROUGH

How hopeful are you in the midst of your "slump" times? Do you trust in the faithfulness of God in the highs and the lows of life? Journal about a time when you trusted in God's faithfulness—in spite of your circumstances.

From the Playbook: Read and meditate on Psalm 42.

TOP 25 GREAT BASEBALL GAMES

THE BOONE IDENTITY   October 16, 2003, New York Yankees 6, Boston Red Sox 5—Add Aaron Boone to the names of relatively obscure players who have broken the hearts of Red Sox fans. Boone did it in Game 7 of the 2003 ALCS when he smacked a Tim Wakefield pitch over the left-field wall for a game-winning home run that gave the Yankees a 6-5 win and another trip to the Fall Classic. Boone's brother Bret was a guest announcer for Fox Sports that day, so America got to share this magnificent moment with Aaron's big brother.

65. CURSES!

"We have been made holy through the sacrifice of the body of Jesus Christ once for all." HEBREWS 10:10

I have a suggestion for fans of the Chicago Cubs. Embrace the curse! It's the only way. Since 1908, the Cubs have been finding amazing ways to avoid winning. They blame it on a curse.

In 1945, a man paid for two seats to a World Series game at Wrigley Field between the Cubs and the Detroit Tigers. That would have been fine, but the second seat was for a goat. Cubs' officials booted them both out of the Friendly Confines. That's when it gets sticky. According to legend, the jilted fan put a curse on the team. The Cubs lost, and they haven't been to a Series since.

FAST FACT:
Wrigley Field, the Cubs' home since 1914, has hosted the World Series five times (1929, 1932, 1935, 1938, 1945).

I say face the curse head-on. Buy a goat and give him a place to graze in the bullpen—which, of course, will have to be renamed. Hey, if the Boston Red Sox can break the Babe Ruth Curse, why can't the Cubs get it done?

What is the official theological position of Discovery House Publishers on all this? Sure, we believe in the curse—and we're all under it. Read on.

Long ago, the first man and woman rebelled against God (Genesis 3:1–6). Because of that, the human race began to die, just as God had warned (2:17).

God's justice demanded that someone pay for our sins. God's love showed us that He had someone in mind all along—His own Son. Jesus became our once-for-all sacrifice

(Hebrews 10:10) when He died on the cross and rose from the dead.

We who trust in Jesus are no longer under the curse of sin and death (John 3:17). We are being "made holy" through His sacrifice (Hebrews 10:14). The curse of sin has been lifted!

Now, if only the Cubs could get out from whatever is stopping them.

—TIM GUSTAFSON

FOLLOW THROUGH

Have you ever thought about the fact that in God's way of looking at things, you are lost and headed for a godless eternity unless your sins are forgiven? Does that make you think more seriously about your view of God and your relationship with Him?

From the Playbook: Read Hebrews 10:1–10.

TOP 25 GREAT BASEBALL GAMES

PERFECTION FOR JOHNSON **May 18, 2004, Arizona Diamondbacks 2, Atlanta Braves 0**—He had been pitching in the major leagues for 17 seasons. He had already struck out more than 4,000 batters. But Randy Johnson saved the best for near the end. At age 40, the big lefthander pitched his first career perfect game, becoming the oldest pitcher to throw such a masterpiece in baseball history. Pitching for the Arizona Diamondbacks against the Atlanta Braves at Turner Field, Johnson struck out 13 Braves hitters in completing the 17th major league perfect game ever.

66. A PROUD FATHER

"You are my Son, whom I love; with you I am well pleased."
LUKE 3:22

On April 6, 2006, Jordan Tata (pronounced TAY-ta) made his major-league debut for the Detroit Tigers. The Plano, Texas, native took the hill with 30 or so of his closest friends and family members rooting him on against the hometown Texas Rangers.

It was a special moment for the 24-year-old pitcher and for his father.

FAST FACT:

Jordan Tata was the Tigers Minor League Pitcher of the Year in 2005 with a stellar 13-2 record at Class A Lakeland. He retired from baseball after the 2009 season.

At the time Ivan Rodriguez, a former Texas Ranger, was the Detroit catcher. He told the *Detroit Free Press*, "My girlfriend told me his parents were crying every time he went out. Every inning. When they took him out of the game, his dad went to his knees and started crying. He was very happy. He was so proud of his son."

This dad's fatherly love for his son is a wonderful picture of earthly love at its deepest. It also gives us a mental image of the most amazing love written of in the Bible—the love between God the Father and Jesus, His Son. (In no way can any earthly father's love for his son or daughter parallel the purity of the love within the Holy Trinity, but the picture is helpful for us to consider.)

In Luke 3:22, we read the powerful words of love that God showered upon His Son, Jesus, following Christ's baptism. At the beginning of Jesus' earthly ministry, God shouted approval and love from the heavens! The timing of this communication of love should not be overlooked. The heavenly Father is giving the Son's future ministry and actions the ultimate endorsement. This holds special significance when you ponder another prominent verse in the New Testament, John 14:6, "I am the way and the truth and the life. No one comes to the Father except through me." —ROB BENTZ

FOLLOW THROUGH

Through prayer, praise God for the amazing gift of His Son, Jesus Christ. Praise God that Jesus is the way, the truth, and the life (John 14:6).

From the Playbook: Read Luke 3.

TOP 25

GREAT BASEBALL GAMES

TWINS TWEAK TIGERS **October 6, 2009, Minnesota Twins 6, Detroit Tigers 5**—Two weeks earlier, the Minnesota Twins' chances seemed over. But they overcame a huge lead by the Tigers to finish in a tie for first. So the teams met in a play-in game for the right to face the Yankees in the ALDS. It was an instant classic as the teams battled for 12 innings. There were plays at the plate, close calls by umpires, and several come-from-behind efforts. In the end, an Alexi Casilla single brought home the game winner for the Twins in the bottom of the 12th as the Tigers' collapse was sealed.

67. FORGIVE AND REMEMBER

*"Who is a God like you, who pardons sin
and forgives the transgression of the remnant
of his inheritance?"* MICAH 7:18

Joshua Canales sent a line drive sizzling down the third base line. His teammate and friend Kelsey Osborn never saw it coming.

The ball struck the 20-year-old infielder above the right ear. He went into convulsions and then slipped into a coma. Six days later, Kelsey was dead.

Joshua couldn't believe it! How could this happen? The two young men had become fast friends while playing for the Newark Raptors of the Northeastern League.

Soon after the tragedy, Kelsey's dad approached Joshua, gave the hurting young man a hug, and told him he loved him. Joshua cried and expressed his remorse.

FAST FACT:

The highest level of minor-league ball Josh reached was AAA with the Las Vegas 51s.

"I thought about never picking up a bat again," Josh recalled later. "But Kelsey's parents told me that if Kelsey knew I was quitting, he would be upset with me."

Joshua was energized by the forgiveness of Kelsey's parents—and he forgave himself. Reluctantly, he moved on, and just a year after the accident, he was drafted in the 16th round of the major league draft by the Los Angeles Dodgers. After finishing up his minor-league career with the Dodgers, Canales became a pastor and a leader of the Fellowship of Christian Athletes in the Los Angeles area.

Forgiveness comes directly from the heart of God. The

prophet Micah, speaking out against the sins of ancient Israel, wrote of Yahweh, "who pardons sin and forgives the transgression of the remnant of His inheritance" (Micah 7:18).

The prophet looked to the future with hope and proclaimed, "You do not stay angry forever but delight to show mercy" (v. 18). Micah knew that God wouldn't hold past sins against His people if they repented.

God forgives you when you confess to Him your sins. But, as Josh did, you must also forgive yourself. If you hang on to the errors of yesterday, you can't serve Jesus with your whole heart today.

Remember the good of the past. Remember God's forgiveness. Forgive yourself.   —TOM FELTEN

FOLLOW THROUGH

What are you having a hard time forgiving yourself for? Do you think God has a hard time forgiving you for anything that you confess?

From the Playbook: Read Micah 7:17–19.

TOP 25 GREAT BASEBALL GAMES

PEREZ WINS IT   **July 11, 1967, National League 2, American League 1**—The 1967 All-Star Game was played at Anaheim Stadium, home of the Angels. It was a pitcher's duel throughout with just two home runs scoring the only runs in the game's first nine innings. Dick Allen hit one for the NL, and Brooks Robinson hit one for the AL in the sixth. The scored stayed that way until Tony Perez stepped to the plate in the sixteenth. Facing Jim "Catfish" Hunter, Perez blasted a home run in the top of the inning. Tom Seaver came in and closed the game by pitching the bottom of the inning. Surprisingly, the game lasted only 3 hours and 41 minutes.

68. CUTTING OUT SHORTCUTS

Game Plan:
Practicing spiritual disciplines

"If anyone would come after me, he must deny himself and take up his cross daily and follow me." LUKE 9:23

After some seasons of ignoring the problem, and some seasons of dealing with surviving the problem, major league baseball now operates under an amphetamine ban. Outlawing amphetamines was significant in that it forbids a stimulant that many major leaguers reportedly have relied on for more than half a century to endure the long summer season. But amphetamines, as well as any potentially performance-enhancing drugs, are nothing more than an attempted shortcut to success.

FAST FACT:
Amphetamines became popular in baseball in the late 1940s after some players who had been given them as soldiers in WWII started using them in the sport.

Shortcuts aren't limited to baseball. In the spiritual realm, people have been trying shortcuts for centuries. In fact, whole religions have been concocted by people trying to find what they think is an easy way to God.

The Bible tells the story of a shortcut artist, Simon the Sorcerer, in Acts 8. After seeing Peter and John miraculously impart the Holy Spirit to some believers, Simon offered the apostles money in exchange for this power, earning a harsh rebuke from Peter.

Simon wanted one-stop shopping for spiritual greatness, but there is no such thing. In Luke 9:23, Jesus said a true believer must "take up his cross daily and follow me," a picture of continual sacrifice. In fact, the biblical doctrine of sanctification, which Jesus (John 17:17), Peter (1 Peter 1:2) and Paul (2 Thessalonians 2:13) all spoke of, is a lifelong process that all Christians must undergo for spiritual maturity. Sure, becoming a Christian is an instantaneous change for the person who puts his or her trust in Jesus, but the process of reaching spiritual maturity takes a lifetime.

Just like the star ballplayer must continually take batting practice and field grounders to stay sharp, so the Christian must constantly practice his or her calling with prayer, Scripture reading, and service.

Don't look for spiritual shortcuts. There are none.

—JOSHUA COOLEY

FOLLOW THROUGH

What are the areas you are not devoting enough time to in your spiritual life? Prayer? Reading the Word? Going to church? Spending time with your spouse? Reflect on your findings and create a plan for change.

From the Playbook: Read John 17.

TOP 25 GREAT BASEBALL GAMES

THE D-BACKS SHOCK THE YANKS   **November 4, 2001, Arizona Diamondbacks 3, New York Yankees 2**—In a World Series moved into November by the events of 9/11, the Arizona Diamondbacks and the New York Yankees offered a bit of everything. There were two blowouts by Arizona (9-1 in Game 1 and 15-2 in Game 6), there were three D-Back-crushing home runs off their reliever Byung-Hyun Kim in two games, and there was a huge comeback win in Game 7. The Yanks led 2-1, and they had Mariano Rivera on the mound. That usually meant a Yankee win. Not this time. After pitching a scoreless eighth, Mo ran into trouble in the ninth. Tony Womack doubled off Rivera to send Midre Cummings home with the tying run. Luis Gonzalez looped a single to score Jay Bell and give the D-Backs their first World Series championship.

69. WHAT MY PLAYER CAN DO

Game Plan:
Using your God-given gifts

"Each one should use whatever gift he has received to serve others." 1 PETER 4:10

During major league baseball's Hot Stove League—you know, that time of the year when baseball general managers and player agents deal with players' lives and family movement as though they were trading cards—a player's physical gifts are always trumpeted loudly. Agents make no secret of the amazing skill sets their players possess. And when a team signs a player, the team trumpets those skills as well.

FAST FACT:
How much does baseball pay for the gifts of a player? The average salary in 2010 was $3.3 million.

When a veteran outfielder inks a $70 million deal, all the media hears from the team's front office is how great the player's gifts are. He can hit. He can run. He's got power. He'll shore up the team's outfield. And on and on it goes.

When a well-traveled pitcher inks a fat contract, the team that signs him can't get the word out fast enough of what a quality pitcher he is and the extra gift that he'll bring to the clubhouse—a desire to mentor the team's young relievers.

During the free-agent shopping and signing period, every player has gifts—and lots of them! (Usually more than the player's previous team ever realized.)

God didn't give gifts just to baseball players. As followers of Christ, you and I have gifts too. While our gifts won't be printed in newspapers or discussed in press conferences aired on ESPN, our gifts hold great significance. The gifts God has given to His followers are for the purpose of serving others for

His glory and honor. The gifts we have are not to be hoarded but to be distributed through love, words, and good deeds. God desires that we would give our gift(s) away!

Every believer has been given at least one gift for His use—and we're not talking about the gift of a 100-mph fastball. Are you using your gift?

—ROB BENTZ

FOLLOW THROUGH

In prayer, ask God to give you three opportunities to use your gifts this week. Then journal about how you used your God-given gifts to serve others. What did you learn from that experience?

From the Playbook: Read 1 Peter 4:1–11.

TOP 25
GREAT BASEBALL GAMES

COBB SAVES THE TIGERS **September 30, 1907, Detroit 9, Philadelphia 9**—The Philadelphia A's and the Detroit Tigers were battling for first place in the American League. The A's came to Bennett Park in Detroit and on the last game of the series were scheduled to play a doubleheader against the Tigers. In Game 1, the A's took a 7-1 lead, but the Tigers battled back in the eighth, Ty Cobb hit a two run home run to tie the game at 8-8. The teams went on to play 17 innings until darkness fell. The game was declared a tie, the second game was cancelled, and Detroit took off for Washington, where they beat the last-place Senators four straight times to end up winning the AL by a game and a half over the A's.

70. WHAT PETE ROSE CAN'T GET

Game Plan:
Realizing that only Jesus can save us from sin

*"But God demonstrates his own love for us in this:
While we were still sinners, Christ died for us."*
ROMANS 5:8

During his professional baseball career, Pete Rose made 17 All-Star teams, was named National League MVP in 1973, and received virtually every Major League Baseball honor awarded. But one thing is missing from his trophy case: A plaque from the Baseball Hall of Fame.

Although Rose deserved to enter the prestigious Hall based on his statistics and his contributions to the game, he has been denied entry because he was caught gambling on baseball—an act baseball has no tolerance for. Major League Baseball not only stripped Rose of his chance to be remembered through the Hall of Fame as one of the all-time greatest baseball players but they also permanently banned him from playing, coaching, or managing a major-league team.

FAST FACT:

Pete Rose is the all-time major-league leader in hits with 4,256. Only he and Ty Cobb (4,191) had more than 4,000 hits.

Many people approach getting into heaven the way Rose approached getting into the baseball Hall of Fame. They imagine there's a list somewhere with all the good things they've done, and that will be sufficient to usher them into God's kingdom. But the Bible says our deeds are like "filthy rags" (Isaiah 64:6). In other words, no matter how many good things we do, we've also done and thought enough sinful things (actually one is enough) that we deserve to be permanently banned from God's presence.

But each of us has available one advantage from God that Rose has not been given yet by baseball: Forgiveness.

Romans 5:8 explains: "But God demonstrates his own love for us in this: While we were still sinners, Christ died for us." That means that even though our sin should keep us out of God's perfect heaven, if we trust Jesus and ask for His forgiveness, our ban from heaven will be lifted. Though we don't deserve it, we can enjoy eternal gain because of Jesus' pain.

—ROXANNE ROBBINS

FOLLOW THROUGH

Today write a "letter to the Lord," thanking Him for sending Christ to pay for your sins.

From the Playbook: Read Romans 5:10–21.

TOP 25 GREAT BASEBALL GAMES

HADDIX: NEARLY PERFECT **May 26, 1959, Milwaukee Braves 2, Pittsburgh Pirates 0**—Never has someone done so well in a baseball game, only to get nothing for it. Pittsburgh's Harvey Haddix retired the first 36 Milwaukee Braves batters he faced—pitching 12 perfect innings. Problem was, Lew Burdette was shutting out the Pirates. In the bottom of the 13th, Don Hoak's error allowed the Braves to get their first base runner. Haddix still had his no-hitter until Joe Adcock hit a home run to end the game. For many years, the game was counted as a perfect game, but in 1991, it was taken off the list because Haddix didn't finish the game without allowing a base runner.

71. CUTTING SOME SLACK

Game Plan:
Appreciating God's mercy

"Mercy triumphs over judgment!" JAMES 2:13

For years, major league baseball operated under a growing cloud of suspicion. A number of players were thought to have used performance-enhancing drugs during the 1990s and decades surrounding it. Then, in 2007, the infamous Mitchell Report was published, and it fingered some of the biggest names in baseball for taking performance-enhancing drugs. While major-league officials and players continue to argue over who took what during the so-called "steroids era," this period is viewed by many as the "dark ages" of America's favorite summer pastime.

FAST FACT:
The Mitchell Report implicated seven former league MVPs as steroid users.

People who love the game of baseball are understandably upset. As one fan put it, "It's dishonest. An honest day's pay for an honest day's work should apply in baseball as well."

It wasn't easy for the majority of players who played by the rules. These guys had to bat, field, and pitch against players who were juiced up and who had bodies that were clearly stronger. The clean players can make a strong case that the unfair competitive advantage steroids created robbed them of the chance at a better performance and a more lucrative contract.

Many believe that those who did use steroids should get everything they deserve. And perhaps they should.

But before we get too far down the road of throwing the book at them, let's remember the universal truth that all of us deserve judgment. We may have never cheated in a sport, but we all have "sinned and fall short of the glory of God"

(Romans 3:23). We all deserve death, sin's wages (Romans 6:23). Thankfully, God is "rich in mercy" (Ephesians 2:4)—and He has provided forgiveness for our sins.

While it's important to hold people accountable for their actions, remembering our own need for mercy frees us to cut others some slack. —JEFF OLSON

FOLLOW THROUGH

Where is it especially hard for you to show mercy? Could that be a symptom of something deeper?

For Further Study: Check out the Discovery Series booklet *When Anger Burns* by going to www.discoveryseries.org.

TOP 25 GREAT BASEBALL GAMES

DODGERS FINALLY WIN ONE **October 4, 1955, Brooklyn Dodgers 2, New York Yankees 0**—Sportswriter Shirley Povich started his World Series recap article on October 5, 1955 with these words: "Please don't interrupt, because you haven't heard this one before. Brooklyn Dodgers, champions of the baseball world. Honest." On the strength of Johnny Podres' shutout of the Yanks in Game 7, and bolstered by a superb outfield catch by Sandy Amoros of a Yogi Berra drive, the Dodgers held on to beat New York 2-0 in the third World Series meeting of the two New York teams in four seasons. For the first time ever, the Bums from Brooklyn sat atop the baseball world.

72. THE POWER OF EXAMPLE

Game Plan:
Leading others to the Savior

"Follow my example, as I follow the example of Christ."
1 CORINTHIANS 11:1

Longtime major-league manager Jim Leyland knows a thing or two about leadership. He has won Manager of the Year awards several times, and he has led two different teams to the World Series (Florida and Detroit). He has managed more than 3,000 major-league games.

During the major-league winter meetings one year, Leyland met with the press and discussed his views on leadership in the big league clubhouse. Leyland said, "I've never yet seen a guy hit .200 who was a leader. A leader's a guy who shuts the other team down when he pitches and knocks in big runs and gets two-out base hits. Those are the guys who are leaders, to me."

As far as we know, Leyland makes no claims to Christianity, but he does paint a picture of what the Bible teaches about authentic leadership. To truly be a leader, God's Word says, we must lead by example.

A baseball player who regularly hits .300, with 30 home runs and 100 runs batted in, will always be a leader to a group of struggling hitters. Teammates will examine his approach at the plate. They will copy his swing. They will seek to follow his lead.

This lead-by-example style is similar to the picture of leadership we read in the words of the apostle Paul. He exhorted others to follow his example as he sought to follow the example of Jesus. Why? Because Jesus' earthly ministry was based on both His words and a life of perfection. Jesus lived it! And Paul wanted others to follow His example.

Leadership is not mere talk—it's example. Our lives should exhibit the reality of our faith. Are you leading others to Jesus with the example of your life? Be a leader. —ROB BENTZ

FOLLOW THROUGH

Examine your life today. Ask God in prayer to make your actions at work/school/home an example of the reality of your faith.

From the Playbook: Read Ephesians 3.

TOP 25 GREAT BASEBALL GAMES

MORRIS THE TIGER **June 8, 1996, LSU 9, Miami 8**—Omaha, Nebraska: College World Series. Championship game. The Miami Hurricanes led the LSU Tigers by a run in the bottom of the ninth 8-7. With two outs, the Tigers managed to get a runner aboard. Up stepped Warren Morris, who had been injured much of the season and had no home runs. He connected and drove the ball over the right field fence to hand the Tigers the College World Series championship. Morris' drive was the first such game-winning home run in CWS history. For his effort, Morris won an ESPY Award and a shot at the majors, where he played for five seasons.

73. COME ON, UMP!

"Always be prepared to give an answer to everyone who asks you to give a reason for the hope that you have." 1 PETER 3:15

Was the runner safe or out? Did the batter beat the throw to first base? Was the pitch a strike or a ball? Was the ball fair or foul? These are the kinds of situations that would bring a major-league manager charging out of the dugout to argue a call.

FAST FACT:

Billy Martin managed five teams (Minnesota, Detroit, Texas, New York Yankees, and Oakland) between 1969 and 1982. He was booted out of 45 games during his managerial career.

As a kid, I would bust a gut watching the antics of a baseball manager arguing a call. One of my all-time favorite arguers was manager Billy Martin, who was hired and fired by the New York Yankees five times in his tumultuous career. I still recall times when he would get so worked up over a "bad" call that he would kick dirt on the umpire's shoes. Of course, that never caused the umpire to reverse his decision, and it always triggered Billy's immediate ejection from the game.

Questioning an umpire's call is as much of a part of America's favorite summer pastime as hot dogs and the seventh-inning stretch. Either as a spectator or a player, all of us, at one time or another, have said, "Come on, ump! What kind of a call was that?"

As long we don't let anger get the best of us and we are not abusive or insulting, there can be a place for arguing a call. But we can take it too far and end up hurting our cause.

Think about something else that can cause people to argue: Matters of faith. When we are talking to an unbeliever about Jesus and Christianity, there can be some intense disagreements. But this is not the time to be confrontational.

Make it your goal to present your "arguments" about your faith in Jesus without being argumentative. Be prepared to give an answer, but also let Christ's love rule what you say as you defend the faith.   —JEFF OLSON

FOLLOW THROUGH

Are you ready to explain your faith to anyone who asks? Can you argue your point without growing agitated?

For Further Study: Check out www.discoveryseries.org and read the booklet *How Can I Share My Faith Without An Argument?*

TOP 25 GREAT BASEBALL GAMES

DODGERS-PHILLIES REDUX   September 30, 1951, Brooklyn 9, Philadelphia 8—For the third straight season, a game between the Dodgers and Phillies would decide the pennant. This time, the Dodgers were holding on after a huge collapse; they were trying to hang on to a tie with the NY Giants, who had already won their game. It was lose and go home for Brooklyn. On this night in Philadelphia, Jackie Robinson saved the day for the Bums and got them into the one-game playoff against the Giants. With the score tied, Robinson made a diving catch in the 12th inning to save the game. In the 14th, he hit a home run to win the game and keep the Dodgers alive for one more game. Bobby Thomson and his date with history awaited.

74. DO THE RIGHT THING

"Anyone, then, who knows the good he ought to do and doesn't do it, sins." JAMES 4:17

In his book *Eight Men Out*, Eliot Asinof records the events surrounding the notorious "Black Sox" baseball scandal of 1919. Eight members of the Chicago White Sox baseball club were accused of taking bribes from gamblers in exchange for intentionally losing the World Series to the Cincinnati Reds, who took the Series five games to three. Although those players were never convicted in a court of law, all eight of the accused were banned from baseball for life. Among the most famous of those players was "Shoeless" Joe Jackson—one of the players who shows up on the Iowa baseball field in the movie *Field of Dreams*.

FAST FACT:
Kenesaw Mountain Landis was baseball commissioner from 1921 through 1944.

Another the Black Sox players, Buck Weaver, claimed that he had played to win despite knowing about the conspiracy. Although Weaver's performance on the field supported his contention (he hit .324 with four doubles and had no errors at third base), baseball commissioner Kenesaw Mountain Landis (who was hired by baseball owners to clean up this mess) ruled that any player who had knowledge of the scandal yet chose not to stop it would still be banned. Weaver was not punished for doing wrong but for failing to do right.

In his letter to the first-century church, James wrote, "Anyone, then, who knows the good he ought to do and doesn't do it, sins" (4:17). In a world filled with evil and darkness, followers of Christ have the opportunity to shine their light.

That often means that when evil rears its head, we must resist the urge to do nothing.

When faced with the choice between doing good and failing to do anything at all, we must always choose to do what's right.

—BILL CROWDER

FOLLOW THROUGH

What error or wrong have you seen recently that you would like to do something about? What is your action plan?

From the Playbook: Read James 4:13–17.

TOP 25 GREAT BASEBALL GAMES

RIPKEN, BOGGS GO 33 **April 18, 1981, Pawtucket 3, Rochester 2**—The longest major-league game ever went 27 innings. But in 1981, a minor-league baseball game between the Pawtucket PawSox and the Rochester Red Wings surpassed that by six innings. The game was so long, it took three days. The game began on Saturday night the 18th of April, was suspended at 4:07 a.m. on the 19th, and finally ended on June 23. On the 23rd, the teams ended the game in just one inning, with the PawSox winning 3-2. Several future major leaguers played in the game, including Cal Ripken Jr., Wade Boggs, Bobby Ojeda, Steve Grilli, and Marty Barrett. One batter, Dallas Williams, went 0-for-13 in the game.

75. SWEENEY'S SURRENDER

"I press on to take hold of that for which Christ Jesus took hold of me." PHILIPPIANS 3:12

During his prime, first baseman Mike Sweeney became one of the best hitters in the majors. "Became" is a key word. It took work. It took discipline. It took being broken.

Listen to Mike as he shares his journey of those first few years.

"Rumors of being traded. Rumors of another trip to AAA. These were the headlines that jumped off the newspaper at me in the spring of 1999. My dreams were slipping away, and I couldn't stop them. Baseball was a driving force in my life, and I always strived to be the hardest worker on the team. Unfortunately, my hard work was not getting me very far.

FAST FACT:

Mike Sweeney banged out more than 1,500 hits and more than 200 home runs in his major-league career.

"The Lord had been a motivating factor in my life. At one time I pictured in my mind the two of us riding on a tandem bike. But now, as I saw my dreams slipping away, this image came to mind again. I was hit with this thought—the steering takes place on the front of a tandem bike. I was on the wrong seat!

"This realization drove me to my knees, and I started bawling my eyes out! I confessed to the Lord that I had never totally surrendered all of myself to Him and given Him control. That day I embraced Jesus as Lord, and when I got up I was a new creature in Christ!"

Are you looking for someone to become the driving force in your life? Are you looking for something to fill that void that only a Savior can fill? Are you looking for something to give you the joy that has always seemed elusive? Do you want to know you are loved, just for who you are in Christ and not because of any accomplishments or accolades?

Do what Mike did. Turn your life over to Jesus. Surrender it all to Him!

—TIM CASH

FOLLOW THROUGH

What is keeping you from surrendering everything to Jesus? Is there something you are holding onto that you are afraid to let go?

From the Playbook: Read Romans 12:1–8.

TOP 25 GREAT BASEBALL GAMES

SPEED BALL **September 28, 1919, New York Giants 6, Philadelphia A's 1**—Can you imagine getting the family together, putting them in the car, driving them to the old ball park, paying for tickets—and having the game end in less time than it takes to conduct a church service? That's the scenario when the New York Giants visited the Philadelphia A's in 1919. The Giants got in, got six runs, got the win, and got out in 51 minutes. Surprisingly, there were 18 hits in the game, three walks, and an error. There were also no pitching changes.

76. YOU'RE NOT TIM TEBOW!

Game Plan:
Presenting the gospel to others

"Go into all the world and preach the good news to all creation." MARK 16:15

Let's face it. There aren't many of us who are anything like Tim Tebow. His high school football stats set him apart from most of us. And then he went to college and became one of the best quarterbacks ever. And then the NFL came calling. Tebow is a remarkable athlete.

But just because he's a great athlete and we're not doesn't mean we can't participate in athletic events.

For instance, if you like to play a little fun football now and then, when your family is together for Thanksgiving and somebody says, "Hey, let's play some touch football in the backyard," you don't say, "Nah, I can't. I'm not as good as Tim Tebow."

FAST FACT:
In 2010, the NCAA banned messages on eyeblack worn by college football players. It's been called the "Tebow Rule," because Tim Tebow put Bible verses on his eyeblack while playing for Florida.

That would be ridiculous.

Similarly, it would be ridiculous to decide that you can't present the gospel to anyone because you don't have Tebow's preaching skills. Sure, he's been known to preach to 10,000 students at one time in the Philippines. But that doesn't make him different from any of us when it comes to fulfilling the great commission. God has called each of us, in one way or another, to make the gospel known to others.

So, if someone were to say, "You know, I really don't get

this Christian stuff. What's the deal?" we can't say, "Uh, I really can't talk about it. I'm not as good as Tim Tebow."

The gospel is the best news that ink has ever printed. It is the plan of God, meant to give life and hope and eternity to everyone who believes. And in God's plan, there is a simple marketing plan to let others know—one person telling another.

Sometimes, a person comes along who can tell thousands at once, and we can be grateful that happens. But that should never cause us to diminish our own responsibility to preach the gospel wherever we are—even if we can just do it one person at a time.

—DAVE BRANON

FOLLOW THROUGH

What are some situations when you are called on to share the gospel? What helps you most to have the courage to do that? How can God's Word give you strength for that task?

From the Playbook: Read 1 Corinthians 9:15–18.

GREAT FOOTBALL GAMES

FOURTH QUARTER MAYHEM   February 1, 2004, New England Patriots 32, Carolina Panthers 29—Two years earlier, the Carolina Panthers had finished 1-15. But in 2004, they earned their way into the Super Bowl against the New England Patriots. The game bumped along until the fourth quarter, with the Patriots holding a 14-10 lead. But in the fourth, both teams scored more points than they had in the previous three. The Pats scored first to make it 21-10. The Panthers roared back to score twice—each time missing attempts for two extra points. That gave them a 22-21 lead with 6:53 left. The Pats scored again and tacked on the two-pointer to lead 29-22. Carolina answered, and the game was tied at 29. Then, with just four seconds left, Adam Vinatieri kicked the game winner, and the Patriots left Houston with the Super Bowl trophy.

77. YOU DO WHAT ON SUNDAY?

Game Plan:
Worshiping Jesus everywhere

"Worship the Lord with gladness." Psalm 100:2

One January, as my team at the time, the Baltimore Ravens, prepared for the Super Bowl, I was asked by a reporter to write a daily Super Bowl diary. It gave me a chance to reflect on this huge game.

For instance, as I got ready for the biggest game of my career, I found that I spent most of my time on my knees and not on my cleats. I felt that I had to surrender my insufficient strength and ask God to arm me with strength for the battle before me (Psalm 18:39).

Over the years I've been asked many times, "How can you play football on Sunday?" It was no different as we got ready for the Super Bowl.

My answer has always been this: True worship is envisioning yourself at the throne of God, and it is not confined to the place you might be. The football field becomes my place of worship on Sunday as I give God the glory after each field goal—make or miss.

Right before we took the field for the Super Bowl, I had the privilege of sharing in worship with many believers on my team. As Trent Dilfer led us in prayer, we looked into one another's eyes and truly had confidence. With many of us having our eyes focused on Christ, we worshiped and then went to battle unified.

Few people will ever experience the thrill of playing in and winning a Super Bowl—but we all have the opportunity and privilege to worship God at His throne anytime and anywhere.

We also have the opportunity to join Him in victory over the biggest battle ever—the battle for lost souls.

—MATT STOVER

FOLLOW THROUGH

Where is the best place for you to worship God? Whom do you enjoy worshiping with?

From the Playbook: Read John 4:21–24.

TOP 25 GREAT FOOTBALL GAMES

ON FROZEN TUNDRA   December 31, 1967, Green Bay Packers 21, Dallas Cowboys 17—The Vince Lombardi Legend gets another chapter as Dallas battles Green Bay for the NFL title. In ice-cold Lambeau Field, where game time temperatures were hovering around minus 13 and the wind-chill approached 50-below, two legendary coaches—Lombardi and Tom Landry faced each other. Bart Starr decided the game on a QB sneak for a touchdown with 16 seconds left.

78. ONE SINGLE FAN

Game Plan
Standing up for God

"They neither serve your gods nor worship the image of gold you have set up." DANIEL 3:12

It would have been impossible to do the wave at the college football game between the Washington State Cougars and the San Jose State Spartans in Pullman, Washington, on November 12, 1955.

Why?

Because the paid attendance for this contest was one. Not one hundred thousand, not one thousand, not one hundred.

One.

According to writer Floyd Conner, it seems that a bitter snowstorm made the faithful stay away in droves, leaving a single fan to root his team on.

FAST FACT:
November 12, 1955, is also the day UCLA beat Washington on a last-minute field goal—a date memorialized in the movie Back to the Future.

Although college football games are not usually where this happens, life is full of instances where you have to stand alone. And it is seldom easy.

A few years ago there was a TV commercial in which a nerdy bicyclist mistakenly showed up for a race all decked out in his helmet and racing spandex, only to be met at the starting line by a bunch of grizzly-looking guys on *real* bikes—Harley-Davidsons. Biker guy was all alone because he forgot to "phone first." That's another picture of how it feels when you are all alone.

Despite the inconvenience and the anxiety that standing alone causes, the Bible indicates that those who do stand up for what is right will receive God's approval and help. For instance, it wasn't easy for Shadrach and his two buddies to stand when everybody around them was bowing down to an idol. But they were protected by the Lord.

Although you won't face a fiery furnace for your stand, there are consequences. Refusing to participate in fraudulent practices may cost you a job. Espousing creation might raise the ire of a science instructor. Witnessing might anger fellow workers. Standing alone and standing out is tough, but it might be the only way to show others that you're not afraid of standing up for God.

—DAVE BRANON

FOLLOW THROUGH

Have you had a tough "stand alone" situation recently? How did you handle it? How could you have handled it better?

From the Playbook: Read Daniel 3.

TOP 25 GREAT FOOTBALL GAMES

THE BAND'S ON THE FIELD **November 20, 1982, California 25, Stanford 20**—John Elway had just led Stanford downfield for what was surely the game-winning field goal. The Cardinal led 20-19 after the three-pointer, and all that was left was the kickoff, a tackle, and a celebration. The kickoff to California was squibbed to avoid a runback. But Stanford didn't anticipate seeing four laterals and then watching Mariet Ford still alive and heading for the end zone with the ball. And Ford didn't anticipate running past not only Cardinal defenders but Stanford fans and the Stanford band, which was making its way onto the field. In the wildest finish of any football game ever, Ford plowed over a trombone player as he dashed past the goal line to give the Bears an improbable 25-20 victory.

79. ONLY WAY TO TURN

"Set your minds on things above, not on earthly things."
COLOSSIANS 3:2

Imagine that you're an 8-year-old with dreams of playing pro ball one day.

Imagine that you are gifted in football and you have a great high school and college career.

Imagine that you then become the first African-American to start at quarterback in the NFL.

Imagine 20 years later being homeless and living on the streets.

Stop imagining. It happened.

Just a few years ago, former Pittsburgh Steelers quarterback Joe Gilliam Jr. was discovered begging on the streets of Nashville. His life, since leaving the game back in 1975 after four seasons, was difficult. His police record—several arrests—is more imposing than his football records are impressive.

FAST FACT:

Sadly, Joe Gilliam Jr. died of a heart attack on Christmas Day 2000— four days before his 50th birthday.

How does someone sink so low? "Sometimes I like myself and sometimes I don't," said Joe, who admitted to continued drug abuse.

Then he said, "Only God can help."

A long time ago, another man needed help—Amaziah, king of Judah. He had made the bad choice to hire 100,000 Israelite mercenaries to do battle for him. But a man of God told him this was wrong and that "the Lord can give you much more than that" (2 Chronicles 25:9).

Amaziah listened and obeyed. At first. But a short time

later he began worshiping pagan idols. His life became a nightmare. First he lost his throne—then his life.

Joe Gilliam Jr. was right when he said, "Only God can help." But recognizing who God is (which King Amaziah did at one time) and choosing to obey Him are two different things.

If you want to keep your life in the game and out of the gutter, set your mind on things above. Strive to obey God. He will give you so much more than anything the world can offer.

—TOM FELTEN

FOLLOW THROUGH

Take your biggest problem and give it to God. Write a note to yourself about this, seal it, and don't look at it for a week. Then open it and see how God has helped you with it.

From the Playbook: Read 2 Chronicles 25.

GREAT FOOTBALL GAMES

THE REICH STUFF   January 3, 1993, Buffalo Bills 41, Houston Oilers 38—Frank Reich had already pulled off the biggest come-from-behind win in college history when he was at Maryland. Now it was the big time, and he did it again. While quarterbacking the Buffalo Bills, Reich faced a 35-6 deficit heading into the second half against the Houston Oilers. When the dust had settled, Reich's Bills had won the game 41-38—the biggest comeback in NFL history.

80. WHY WALK AWAY?

"As we have opportunity, let us do good to all people, especially to those who belong to the family of believers." GALATIANS 6:10

Napoleon Kaufman was just 27 years old when he walked away from professional football in 2000.

His body wasn't injured. His million-dollar contract was in place for the 2001 season, so there were no contract "issues" to get hammered out. Napoleon's Oakland Raiders were coming off an AFC West championship season, and the team was primed to be one of the best in the conference again in the upcoming season—with a legitimate shot at the Super Bowl. And Kaufman had plenty of individual success in the NFL, rushing for more than 1,000 yards during the 1997 season.

FAST FACT:

You can find out more about Pastor Napoleon Kaufman and his church at www .thewellchurch.net.

So exactly what was it that pulled the former University of Washington star away from the gridiron? The answer might surprise you. It was Napoleon's passion for ministry!

Kaufman's agent, Cameron Foster, told ESPN, "He loves football, but I guess he loves ministering more."

Kaufman, known in college for his speed, shifty moves, and hard-charging lifestyle, gave his life to Jesus Christ after he began his NFL career. After that, he become an ordained minister, and he sought to let the love of Jesus Christ flow through him and into the lives of others as the pastor of a California church. Obviously, Napoleon believed he could do that more effectively by not playing football.

As Christians, we should all have a similar passion for reaching out and ministering to others.

In the gospel of Matthew, our Lord Jesus told the disciples about reaching out to those in need. He said, "whatever you did for one of the least of these brothers of mine, you did for me" (25:40).

Perhaps that's why Napoleon loves ministering so much, because he knows he's serving his Savior. —ROB BENTZ

FOLLOW THROUGH

Volunteer one hour of your time each week for the next month to your church or to a local ministry.

From the Playbook: Read Matthew 25:31–46.

TOP 25 GREAT FOOTBALL GAMES

A MODEST PROPOSAL **January 1, 2007, Boise State 43, Oklahoma 42**—All Boise State wanted to do was to suggest that they were among the best in college football. All Ian Johnson wanted to do was win the game and ask his girlfriend to marry him. With a lot of skill, a little trickery, and a national TV audience to watch it all unfold, the Broncos made it all happen. In the final seconds of regulation, Boise State scored on an old-fashioned hook-and-ladder play. Then, in overtime, after scoring a TD to pull within one of the Sooners, the Broncos went for the two-point conversion. They pulled off a perfect Statue of Liberty play as Ian Johnson scampered into the end zone for the 43-42 win over Oklahoma. That's when he took a knee and proposed to Chrissy Popadics, a Broncos cheerleader. They were married the following summer.

81. HE KEPT GOING AND GOING ...

Game Plan:
Avoiding wrong decisions

"The Lord searches every heart and understands every motive." 1 CHRONICLES 28:9

Seven years is a long time to play college football.

Sure, there are redshirt guys who can squeeze five years out of a scholarship, but they are just rookies compared to Ron Weaver. This guy set a record that will probably never be broken.

He played seven years of college football. Not legally, you understand. First he played two years at a junior college before transferring to Sacramento State for his junior and senior years. That's four years, if you are keeping track. That, of course, is pretty much the limit on the number of college years you can suit up and play one sport.

But hey, when you love football, you just can't stop. Using a "borrowed" social security number and an assumed name to match, "Don't call me Ron" enrolled as a freshman in another junior college, where he played two more years. To help you with the math: that's six years.

Now, if that wasn't gutsy enough, the guy then moved on to the University of Texas—one of the most famous football schools in the land. There, at age 30, he played defensive back for the Longhorns. Finally, as Texas was preparing to play in the 1996 Sugar Bowl, the ruse was discovered, and the long-in-the-tooth Longhorn was sent packing.

Although you can't fault Weaver's dedication, what he did points out a common error: Doing wrong to produce good results. It's the old "going over the speed limit to get to church on time" scenario. Cheating on taxes so the family can afford a new dishwasher just won't wash. It's still wrong, even if good comes from it.

Remember, we might be able to pull the wool over human eyes, but the Lord "understands every motive" (1 Chronicles 28:9).

Doing wrong is never right.   —DAVE BRANON

FOLLOW THROUGH

What have I done wrong that I justified by claiming good motives? Does someone need an apology?

From the Playbook: Read Genesis 12:10–20.

TOP 25 GREAT FOOTBALL GAMES

THE MAGIC FLUTIE   **November 23, 1984, Boston College 47, Miami 45**—The Hurricanes had the previous week succumbed to Frank Reich's big comeback (See No. 79), losing to Maryland 42-40 after leading at the half 31-0. They were not expecting another dagger in the heart. But Doug Flutie delivered just that. After Miami scored to go up 45-41 with 30 seconds left, BC's Flutie got the Eagles to Miami's 48, and he had time for one more play. He stepped back and fired the ball more than 63 yards downfield. Gerald Phelan raced past the Miami secondary and caught the ball as he crossed the goal line for the win.

82. GOING THE RIGHT WAY?

Game Plan:
Following the path to eternal life

"Narrow the road that leads to life, and only a few find it." MATTHEW 7:14

Jim Marshall is one of the NFL's all-time great defensive ends. Drafted by the Cleveland Browns in the second round of the 1960 NFL Draft, Marshall played 20 NFL seasons (1960–1979) starting a record 282 straight games for the Browns and then the Minnesota Vikings. Marshall was a key member of the famed Minnesota "Purple People Eaters" defense.

Marshall played in four Super Bowls and a pair of Pro Bowls during his career. He is a legend in the eyes of Vikings fans who believe the Vikings' iron man should be in the Pro Football Hall of Fame.

FAST FACT:

Marshall's coach with the Vikings, Bud Grant, was inducted into the Pro Football Hall of Fame in the Class of 1994.

Yet for football fans outside of the Twin Cities, Marshall will always be remembered as the guy who went the wrong way. In a game against the San Francisco 49ers on October 25, 1964, Marshall scooped up a fumble and raced 60 yards for a touchdown—or so he thought. But there was a problem. Marshall ran to the wrong end zone! Instead of scoring a touchdown for the Vikings, he scored a safety for the Niners!

Marshall's infamous play serves as a picture of the way many people are currently living their lives. They're heading in the wrong direction—yet they believe they're doing something good. They believe they're going in the right direction.

In Matthew's gospel, Jesus is very direct about the way to go. There is only one way: through the narrow gate. He tells us that the road to eternal life is also narrow. It's so narrow that few actually find it! Few actually enter the gate, and few are on the right path—following Christ.

The wrong road is easier, like Marshall's path to the wrong end zone. Yet it leads to destruction.

Have you entered the gate? Are you on the right path in pursuit of Jesus?   —ROB BENTZ

FOLLOW THROUGH

Read and meditate on the words of Jesus in Matthew 7:13–14. Consider your current path. Have you entered the narrow gate? Have you placed your faith in Jesus for your salvation? If not, you can do so now by talking with God through the words of the following prayer: *Jesus, I want to follow you. I confess my sin and ask you to forgive me. I know your path is narrow, so please give me the power through your Holy Spirit to walk it faithfully. Amen.*

From the Playbook: Read Matthew 7:13–14

TOP 25 GREAT FOOTBALL GAMES

GAME OF THE CENTURY **November 9, 1946, Notre Dame 0, Army 0**—No, this was not a soccer game. It was a showdown between the No. 1 team in the land, Army, and the No. 2 team, Notre Dame. Some called it the Game of the Century. Played at Yankee Stadium before 74,121 football fans, it pitted two 6-0 teams with high-powered offenses. Both teams had Heisman Trophy quarterbacks (Doc Blanchard, Army 1945 and Johnny Lujack, Notre Dame 1947), but neither could muster as much as a field goal. Both teams finished the season undefeated because in 1946 there was no overtime in college football.

83. SAY NO TO IMMORALITY

*"Be very careful, then, how you live—not as unwise
but as wise, making the most of every opportunity,
because the days are evil."* EPHESIANS 5:15–16

Former Cincinnati Bengals linebacker David Pollack played
his college football at the University of Georgia.

As a talented lineman, Pollack attracted the attention of
many publications that named All-American teams. One publication offered Pollack more than just the honor.
This publication wanted to fly him to California,
provide him with posh accommodations, show
him some good times, and, of course, take his picture for inclusion in its preseason All-American
college football preview.

Cool, huh?

Maybe not. This publication is one that has
been attempting to destroy the morals of Americans for the past 50 years. It is one that features
provocative photos of unclothed females—and articles that
promote a lifestyle of godless hedonism. This publication is
Playboy.

FAST FACT:
*David Pollack
played just one
NFL season
before a neck
injury forced
him to retire in
2007.*

The Bible clearly stands diametrically opposed to the sexual revolution pushed by this magazine. Association with this
publication continues to represent connections with ungodliness and immorality.

And Pollack stood his ground. He said, "No" to *Playboy*
and its request for him to be one of its All-Americans. That is
discernment. And it's not easy. He was criticized by many for
turning the magazine down.

"It was nice that they thought enough of me to select me for that honor," Pollack said. "But to me, turning down that 'honor' was a no-brainer."

Look at what Paul says in 1 Thessalonians 4: "It is God's will that you be sanctified: that you should avoid sexual immorality; that each of you should learn to control his own body in a way that is holy and honorable"(vv. 3–4).

The principle is clear: God wants you to live in a way that is "set apart," or "sanctified." And part of that is to be sexually pure.

That's not easy. But it's what God wants and it's what He honors.

—DAVE BRANON

FOLLOW THROUGH

What area in your life needs better discernment on your part? Would it be helpful to enlist a friend for accountability purposes?

From the Playbook: Read Ephesians 5:1–18.

TOP 25 GREAT FOOTBALL GAMES

THE CATCH JR.   February 3, 2008, New York Giants 17, New England Patriots 14—If Dwight Clark's snag was The Catch (see No. 87), David Tyree's is at least The Catch Jr. And while Tyree's incredible snag of Eli Manning's pass did not result in a game-winning TD, it can be seen as pivotal to the Giants' upset of the previously undefeated Patriots. Third and five. Trailing 14-10. A buck 15 left. It was do-or-die time for New York. Shotgun formation. Manning suddenly has three Pats in his face and grabbing his body and uniform. Manning some-how wriggled out and tossed the ball to Tyree, who ended up pinning the ball between his right hand and his helmet. First down. The drive still alive, the Giants went on to score the winner. And Tyree had what some call the greatest catch in Super Bowl history.

84. LASTING SATISFACTION?

Game Plan:
Filling the real void in our lives

"Lord, what do I look for? My hope is in you."
PSALM 39:7

How long do you think the fans stayed content after my team, the Baltimore Ravens, won the Super Bowl on January 28, 2001? It took just one week for someone to ask me, "What about your chances of winning the Super Bowl next year?"

After more than two decades of playing in the NFL and after winning a Super Bowl ring, I have found that the world tries to convince me of several falsehoods.

First, the world tells me that my athletic accomplishments and success on the field will bring me lasting satisfaction—but I know that over time my athletic ability will fade away, and someone will come along to break any records that I left behind.

FAST FACT:
Matt Stover scored more than 2,000 points in his NFL career.

So, where is my hope if it is not in football and the success it brings? Psalm 39:7 says it best. My hope is in God.

Second, the world tells me that my economic success will buy me happiness. In Ecclesiastes, wise King Solomon said that all earthly treasures are empty and meaningless. True happiness comes from knowing God, who tells us that there is no eternal hope or purpose in material things. They are all temporary.

God's viewpoint is drastically different from the world's viewpoint about these and many other subjects. As a Christian, I have found that fulfilling something greater than myself (like the Great Commission, for example) will give my life eternal purpose and satisfaction. I have also found that Jesus alone can fill the void we all have in our lives.

Be prepared when the world tries to sell you the wrong message about true happiness and purpose in life. Don't buy into it!

The truth is, contentment is found in Christ alone.

—MATT STOVER

FOLLOW THROUGH

What have I been depending on recently for happiness? How should I revise my opinion about finding contentment?

From the Playbook: Read Ecclesiastes 4 and 12:13–14.

GREAT FOOTBALL GAMES

MUSIC CITY MIRACLE January 8, 2000, Tennessee Titans 22, Buffalo Bills 16—This was California vs. Stanford without the band. The Bills had this AFC Wild Card playoff game won. Kick and tackle. Game over. Jeff Fisher had a different plan. It was called Home Run Throwback, and it included a long lateral pass during the kickoff return. It worked to perfection, and it ended with Kevin Dyson scampering 75 yards for a touchdown to end Buffalo's season. The Titans made it all the way to Super Bowl XXXIV.

85. ENCOURAGEMENT AND INSTRUCTION

Game Plan:
Developing young leaders

"I remind you to fan into flame the gift of God."
2 TIMOTHY 1:6

In the offseason before the 2010 NFL season, the Carolina Panthers and Philadelphia Eagles made some big moves. After years with veteran quarterbacks Jake Delhomme and Donovan McNabb at the helm of their respective teams, both teams waved goodbye to their veterans. Carolina cut Delhomme and his big-money contract. Philadelphia traded McNabb.

Did either team have a veteran back-up who would be an improvement? No. Did either team sign a high-priced free agent? No. Did they acquire a high-profile quarterback in trade? Nope.

Instead, the Panthers and Eagles committed to a youth movement. They placed their offense—and their football faith—in the hands of youngsters with little game experience.

In Carolina, Matt Moore finished off the 2009 campaign leading the Panthers to a 4-1 record. In Philadelphia, the Eagles gave three-year back-up Kevin Kolb command of their offense. Did these two youngsters handle the job? Could they lead their units? Both teams placed a great deal of confidence in their ability to lead and make good decisions.

The apostle Paul wrote a series of letters known as the pastoral epistles, including the New Testament book known as 2 Timothy. This letter was written to a young man he calls

FAST FACT:
The Eagles selected Kevin Kolb with the 36th pick in the 2007 NFL Draft. Carolina's Matt Moore went undrafted out of Oregon State in the same year.

his "son" in the faith—kind of a backup quarterback in Paul's world of Christian leadership. Throughout the letter, Paul gives Timothy both encouragement and instruction. This is a key pattern for the development of young leaders.

The first chapter is highlighted by Paul's acknowledgement of Timothy's deep faith and Christ-centered heritage (v. 5). Paul uses this to encourage him. Then Paul exhorts Timothy to use, with confidence, his God-given gifts and abilities (v. 6). Paul is giving his young leader clear instruction to live out the reality of his gifts and his calling.

Encouragement and instruction are key elements for the development of any young leader—in football, in faith, or in life!   —ROB BENTZ

FOLLOW THROUGH

If you are a young leader, you would be wise to listen to both the encouragement and instruction of an older leader. This is the biblical model Paul gives us in 1 and 2 Timothy. Who could be your mentor?

From the Playbook: Read 2 Timothy 1:3

TOP 25 GREAT FOOTBALL GAMES

ELWAY BREAKS CLEVELAND'S HEART **January 11, 1987, Denver Broncos 23, Cleveland Browns 20**—Cleveland doesn't get many chances at championships, but on this date, they were six minutes from going to the Super Bowl. The Browns led the visiting Denver Broncos 20-13, and they had backed the Broncos up to their own two-yard line. But Elway marshaled his troops downfield, and they tied the game. In overtime, he did it again, moving the Broncos into field goal range, where Rich Karlis drove a dagger into the hearts of Browns fans everywhere with the game winner: 23-20.

86. THE RIGHT ROLE MODEL

"Let another praise you, and not your own mouth."
PROVERBS 27:2

At one time during his football career, Danny Wuerffel had every reason in the world to "think of [himself] more highly than [he] ought" (Romans 12:3). After all, among the thousands of college athletes who played NCAA football in 1996, Danny Wuerffel was voted the very best player. He was handed the Heisman Trophy as quarterback of the Florida Gators.

Also living in Florida at the time was a little kid whose parents wanted him to look up to the right kind of people.

FAST FACT:
Wuerffel and Tebow sometimes appear together for Fellowship of Christian Athletes activities.

This was a Christian family—a missionary family, actually—and they wanted their little boy Timmy to follow in the footsteps of someone who loved Jesus, who stayed humble, and who played some pretty good football.

So, little Timmy was encouraged to look up to Wuerffel as his role model. Not only did Timmy get a chance to see Wuerffel in action on the gridiron, but he also got the thrilling opportunity to meet him in person. When Timmy approached Danny Wuerffel and asked for his autograph, the best player in college football obliged.

That's what humility does. It reminds a person that he's not too good to help a 7-year-old kid.

Timmy grew up to be Tim Tebow.

Pam Tebow talked about the difference the older quarterback made in the younger quarterback's life.

"Danny Wuerffel taught him a lot about humility," says Pam Tebow, Tim's mom. "He was a wonderful role model, and he never disappointed us."

Here's what Paul said in 1 Corinthians 10: "I try to please everybody in every way. For I am not seeking my own good but the good of many, so that they may be saved" (v. 33). Paul was a role model.

So was Danny Wuerffel. And now Tim Tebow. Are we?

—DAVE BRANON

FOLLOW THROUGH

Make a list of the situations in which you can be a role model to others—representing Christ to them. What can you do in those situations to lead others to ask about what Jesus has done in your life?

From the Playbook: Read 1 Corinthians 10:31–11:1

GREAT FOOTBALL GAMES

NEVER-ENDING STORY   December 25, 1971, Miami Dolphins 27, Kansas City Chiefs 24 (2 overtimes)—In the longest game in NFL history—a game graced by 11 future Hall-of-Famers—Ed Podolak was the star. He accounted for 350 total yards. The game chewed up 82 minutes and 40 seconds of clock time as the teams went back and forth. Garo Yepremian hit the game-winning field goal midway through the second overtime.

87. BE LIKE MIKE ... BROWN

Game Plan:
Going all out for God

"Stand firm in the faith; be men of courage; be strong."
1 CORINTHIANS 16:13

The psalmist said, "I will speak of your statutes before kings and will not be put to shame" (Psalm 119:46). One way to think about what the psalmist is saying to us is to consider this two-word summary: "Don't flinch!"

The dictionary defines the word *flinch* as "to withdraw or shrink from, as if from pain." If we let pain cause us to flinch in our Christian walk, we will definitely lose impact.

FAST FACT:

In his final year with Kansas City in 2009, Mike Brown recorded 103 tackles for the Chiefs.

Football players have to learn not to flinch. One fearless player who had that down was strong safety Mike Brown, who played for the Chicago Bears and the Kansas City Chiefs. I had the opportunity to recruit Mike Brown from Saguaro High School in Arizona to attend the University of Nebraska. Mike was only 5'8" and barely 180 pounds in high school, but he moved around the football field like a rocket! There was never any hesitation when he tackled another player. Not once did I see him flinch when driving his body into a ball carrier.

Not many players tackle like Mike Brown. That's why he is such a great player. Some players, just before they make contact, flinch and turn their head and shoulders a little bit. They don't want to take the full blow. The natural tendency is to wince and avoid pain.

Coaches teach that it's better to initiate the blow at full speed with proper technique than to avoid the contact by flinching.

That is exactly what God wants from us. He needs full-speed players who are willing to think, walk, and talk in a way that helps them live out their relationship with Jesus Christ to a world that opposes them. God wants brave men and women to take on the opposition in the name of Jesus Christ at all costs.

Don't flinch!

—RON BROWN

FOLLOW THROUGH

What makes you want to flinch in your Christian life? Why do you sometimes lack courage? How can your close fellowship with God give you courage not to shrink back—but to attack the challenge?

From the Playbook: Read 2 Timothy 1:1–9.

TOP 25 GREAT FOOTBALL GAMES

DWIGHT'S HEIGHT **January 10, 1982, San Francisco 49ers 28, Dallas Cowboys 27**—Two words belong to Dwight Clark in the annals of NFL history: The Catch. That's all you have to say, and your football friends know that you are referring to Clark's reception of a Joe Montana pass in an NFC Championship game. With less than a minute left and with the ball on the six-yard line, Montana rolled out, expecting to hit Freddie Solomon with the ball. But he was covered, and Ed "Too Tall" Jones was bearing down on him. Montana pumped and fired. The ball seemed to be sailing out of bounds when Clark leaped higher than seem possible and snatched the ball out of the air. He somehow came down in bounds, and the Niners were on the way to Super Bowl XVI.

88. TAKE ONE FOR THE TEAM

"We put up with anything rather than hinder the gospel of Christ." 1 CORINTHIANS 9:12

Free? When we trust Jesus Christ as Savior, aren't we set free? The apostle Paul thought about that question, and with the help of the Holy Spirit, said, "Though I am free and belong to no man, I make myself a slave to everyone."

Our freedom in Christ is not a freedom from relationships. It is a freedom to love as Jesus loves and to give as Jesus gives.

NFL quarterback Jon Kitna showed us how that works.

FAST FACT:

In his NFL career, Kitna passed for more than 27,000 yards and more than 150 touchdowns.

In 2003, Jon Kitna took the Cincinnati Bengals, an NFL team that had been struggling, and guided it to a respectable 8-8 record. He stood behind center for every single offensive snap of the 16-game season, passing for 3,591 yards and 15 touchdowns.

But the success of 2003 was followed by the snub of 2004. The Bengals relegated Kitna to the sidelines and gave Carson Palmer the ball. So how did Kitna, a Christian, respond?

Kitna became Palmer's biggest booster.

How did he do it? How did a guy who had worked so hard to get to the top of his profession handle things with such class?

"The thing that helped me the most in getting over the disappointment of losing my job was Jeremiah 29:11–13,"says Kitna. "That verse clearly states that God has a plan for my life. Since I know that God is in total control of all things—and yes even seemingly trivial things as an NFL depth chart—for me to complain and cause a fuss would really be an indictment of my faith in the living God."

Freedom in Christ does not give us the right to demand our way. Freedom in Christ is so powerful that it allows us to love when others hate, care when others don't, give when others take, forgive when others can't.

"I make myself a slave to everyone," Paul said. Free, but a slave.

Can you do that today in a way that brings glory to God?

—DAVE BRANON

FOLLOW THROUGH

Think about how things are going at work or school or home. Are there any circumstances where you feel that you are being mistreated—but you want to exercise your freedom in Christ to be strong and do the right thing? Have you prayed for God's help with that?

From the Playbook: Read 1 Corinthians 9:1–12.

TOP 25 GREAT FOOTBALL GAMES

THE ORIGINAL "THE CATCH" **December 23, 1972, Pittsburgh Steelers 13, Oakland Raiders 7**—Ten years before Dwight Clark's catch and eight years before David Tyree was born, Franco Harris made a catch that changed the Pittsburgh Steelers forever. Sometimes referred to as the Immaculate Reception, this play allowed the Steelers, who had never won a playoff game, to beat the Oakland Raiders and move to the AFC title game. Terry Bradshaw fired a pass toward John Fuqua, but Jack Tatum hit him as the ball arrived, sending the ball tumbling backwards. Just before it reached the ground, Harris grabbed it and rushed in for a touchdown to give the Steelers their first playoff win ever.

89. A FRESH START

Game Plan:
Understanding repentance

"Repent, for the kingdom of heaven is near." MATTHEW 4:17

Pittsburgh Steelers quarterback Ben Roethlisberger enjoyed plenty of on-field success early in his NFL career. Off the field, the results were a bit different.

The stats on the back of Big Ben's football card are impressive; strong passing numbers, big win totals, and Super Bowl victories. Few fans would argue that Roethlisberger is one of the NFL's best quarterbacks—especially in big game situations.

Yet the same fans who supported his on-field success had to have been shocked at Roethlisberger's life away from the field. His life off the field was sometimes a series of bad decisions and worse behavior.

FAST FACT:

Just 10 quarterbacks have guided their NFL team to two (or more) Super Bowl titles (John Elway, Bob Griese, Jim Plunkett, Bart Starr, Roger Staubach, Troy Aikman, Terry Bradshaw, Joe Montana, Tom Brady, and Ben Roethlisberger).

- In 2006, Roethlisberger was involved in a near fatal motorcycle accident in downtown Pittsburgh. He sustained a number of head and facial injuries because he was not wearing a helmet.
- In 2008 and again in 2010 he was accused of sexual assault.

Neither of the assault charges led to criminal charges being filed, but the 2010 incident led to a six-game suspension by the NFL for a violation of the league's personal conduct policy.

Ben Roethlisberger's boorish behavior almost cost him his life and has certainly damaged his reputation. He has since apologized for his off-field choices and vowed to make personal changes.

Are an apology and an "I'll try to do better" commitment from any of us enough? Or does the Bible teach a different way?

The first words of preaching from the mouths of John the Baptist (Matthew 3:2), Jesus (Matthew 7:14), and the twelve apostles (Mark 6:12) all began with the same message—repent!

The word is not merely a sorrow for sin, but a decisive change—a turning away from sin to begin a new life of obedience. It means to change one's mind so that one's views, values, and actions change as well. To repent means to start a new life in a completely different direction.

Should you do that?

—ROB BENTZ

FOLLOW THROUGH

Repentance is an active beginning step of a major life change. It requires humility before God and a desire to be led by the Holy Spirit in a new way of thinking and living. Should you repent of your sin and place your faith in Jesus?

From the Playbook: Read Matthew 3:1–6.

TOP 25 GREAT FOOTBALL GAMES

LONGHORN SURPRISE **January 4, 2006, Texas 41, USC 38**—Vince Young took over this national championship game late in the fourth quarter. His Texas Longhorns trailed USC 38-26 with 6:42 left as these two undefeated teams battled. In the ensuing drive, Young rushed for 25 yards and passed for 44 to account for all the yardage Texas would need to score and make it 38-33 with 3:58 left. With 2:09 left, Texas took the ball over on downs at their 44. The Longhorns moved the ball to the 14, and Young rushed it in from there to win the national championship for Texas.

90. A HUMBLING EXPERIENCE

Game Plan:
Living in humility

"Clothe yourselves with humility toward one another."
1 PETER 5:5

Do you recall the Green Bay Packers' forgettable season of 2005?

That was the year Brett Favre struggled for the green and gold—perhaps a season he wished he had not stuck around to play. The Packers won just three football games that year. There were few bright moments for the Pack in this post-playoff era campaign.

FAST FACT:
Samkon Gado intends to some-day become a medical mission-ary to his home country of Nigeria.

One was a mighty mite sparkplug of a running back named Samkon Gado—a scampering ball-carrier who ignited the Packers in a number of late-season games with his surprising success.

Here's his story. Grew up in Nigeria. Moved to the United States and attended Liberty University. Played football for the Flames. Started a paltry two games for Liberty. Not surprisingly, when he left Lynchburg, Gado was not drafted by the NFL.

Nigeria. Liberty. Two starts. Not drafted.

Hey, Sam! Welcome to grad school.

Not so fast. As a free agent, Samkon won his way onto the Packers' squad and ended up being the story of the year in Green Bay, rushing for 582 yards and six touchdowns.

What did this do to Gado? Inflate his ego into another NFL big head?

Fortunately, he knew that was a possibility. "I believe it's in every person's nature," he said, "to be overcome with pride."

But Gado is convinced he's not the one who made the NFL happen. When he looks back at the slim-to-none chance he had to stick with the Packers, he says, "I say this is an act of God."

"God opposes the proud but gives grace to the humble" (1 Peter 5:5).

If we do as Samkon Gado did and credit our Maker for making us the way we are, God will bestow on us His grace. Peter goes on to say that God will even "lift you up" (v. 6).

How much better to let God do that than for us to try to lift ourselves up.

That just leads to a big fall.

—DAVE BRANON

FOLLOW THROUGH

While it's good to take pride in a job well done, it's not good to be overly prideful—forgetting where our ability and strength comes from. Are there areas in which pride hampers your testimony for Jesus? How can you rein that in?

Following the Playbook: Read 1 Peter 5:5–7.

GREAT FOOTBALL GAMES

KORDELL CONNECTS **September 24, 1994, Colorado 27, Michigan 26**—The Michigan Wolverines had this one in the bag. They led 26-21 with just six seconds left on the Michigan Stadium clock. Colorado's coach Bill McCartney—a former Michigan assistant and the architect of the 90s phenomenon called Promise Keepers—called Rocket Left. Michael Westbrook, Blake Anderson, and Rae Carruth all lined up to the left and raced down field. Quarterback Kordell Stewart stepped back and fired the football 70 yards downfield. The ball deflected off Anderson and into the waiting hands of Westbrook as the Big House grew quiet and the Buffaloes raced onto the field to celebrate a victory.

91. DOUBLE COVERAGE TROUBLE

Game Plan:
Staying away from trouble

"Avoid every kind of evil." 1 THESSALONIANS 5:22

Anyone who has ever played quarterback—whether you were the star of your high school team or the kid who never passed a football after the glory years of recess in the fifth grade—knows that protecting the ball is crucial. To be a good quarterback, you simply cannot turn the ball over.

Ask any football coach, and he'll tell you that a quarterback who tosses the ball all over the field with little concern for its final destination is no football player he wants anywhere near the backfield!

FAST FACT:

During the 1990 and 1991 NFL seasons, Bernie Kosar threw 308 passes in a row without an interception.

Coaches want the man who goes under center to be cautious with the ball when it is hiked his way. Simply put, the signal-caller needs to protect the rock. That's why we often see NFL quarterbacks lose yardage by taking a sack rather than sailing an errant pass into double coverage. Firing a pass to a player who's being shadowed by two defenders is risky at best—and most likely will lead to an interception.

A football coach views a quarterback's pass into double coverage as an unnecessary evil. Almost nothing good can come from it!

The words of 1 Thessalonians 5:22 remind us as followers of Jesus Christ that we need to avoid real-life situations that are comparable to a quarterback throwing into double coverage. We need to avoid those things that are risky at best—and most likely sinful. We need to avoid throwing ourselves into situations where sin and unhealthy decisions can intercept us.

The next time you face a difficult decision or situation, think like a good quarterback and avoid double coverage. Be cautious. Avoid every kind of evil. —ROB BENTZ

FOLLOW THROUGH

What is your No. 1 source of temptation? What tends to lure you into enemy territory where you could be intercepted by the other side? What steps do you need to avoid that possibility?

From the Playbook: Read Proverbs 16.

TOP 25 GREAT FOOTBALL GAMES

SNOW BOWL   November 25, 1950—Michigan and Ohio State have played each other since 1897, but no game compares with what happened on the banks of the Olentangy River in Columbus in 1950. A blizzard was on the way, and Ohio State could have canceled the game and earned a trip to the Rose Bowl. But they played in horrendous conditions. The teams combined for 45 punts—sometimes on first down. Conditions were so bad that Michigan did not complete a pass nor register a single first down. Yet they won 9-3 on a safety and a TD scored on a blocked punt. Michigan went to Pasadena and beat Cal 14-6 on New Year's Day.

92. LEON'S LAPSE

"Pride goes before destruction, a haughty spirit before a fall."
PROVERBS 16:18

It's a priceless Super Bowl moment. January 31, 1993, at the Rose Bowl in Pasadena, California. Super Bowl XXVII. Dallas Cowboys' defensive lineman Leon Lett had just scooped up a fumble and was lumbering down the field, destined for yet another TD against the hapless Buffalo Bills.

But as large Leon mentally choreographed which dance routine to implement upon his arrival in the end zone, the Bills' Don Beebe was relentlessly chewing up yardage between them. With a lunge, Beebe knocked the ball loose at the one. The pigskin rolled into the end zone and out of bounds. The Bills got the ball at the 20, and Leon Lett got a prominent place in the Super Bowl hall of blunders.

FAST FACT:

Leon's blunder has been ranked No. 1 on ESPN's 25 Biggest Sports Blunders.

Although I'd most like to identify with the no-quit Beebe in this scenario, I'm afraid I've got a lot of Lett-like moments in my past. Hey, everybody! Look at me! Watch what I'm doing! Oops.

Which reminds me of Haman, who wasn't satisfied with his prominent position in Persia. A troublesome Hebrew named Mordecai wouldn't pay him homage. So Haman conspired against not only Mordecai but against every Jewish person in the kingdom. Unbeknownst to Haman, Mordecai was the queen's uncle. Oops.

When the queen pointed out Haman's murderous intentions to the king, Haman wound up swinging from the very gallows he had constructed for Mordecai.

It's a rare person who doesn't struggle with pride. It can be a big problem for all of us. But such an attitude runs counter to the selfless life Jesus modeled for us.

"Pride goes before destruction," says the ancient Middle Eastern wise man, "a haughty spirit before a fall" (Proverbs 16:18). That same sage also wrote, "Let another praise you, and not your own mouth" (27:2).

That's timely advice for the football field—and for the game of life as well. —TIM GUSTAFSON

FOLLOW THROUGH

What motivates me? Honor? Prestige? Greed? What ought to motivate me? What motivated Jesus when He washed His disciples' feet? (John 13:12–17).

From the Playbook: Read Esther 5:9–14, 7:1–10.

GREAT FOOTBALL GAMES

THE NFL ARRIVES   December 28, 1958, New York Giants 23, Baltimore Colts 17—In the first nationally televised NFL game, the sport started off with what some call the Greatest Game Ever. Johnny Unitas led the Baltimore Colts past the New York Giants 23-17 in sudden-death overtime. It was pre-Super Bowl, so the Colts claimed the NFL championship with the win.

93. TENDER MACHO MAN

Game Plan:
Showing Christlike compassion

"Carry each other's burdens, and in this way you will fulfill the law of Christ." GALATIANS 6:2

For LaDainian Tomlinson, the 2004 season ended on a negative note—a 20-17 playoff loss to the New York Jets in December. Yet Tomlinson knew something really good was about to happen.

He was about to be a daddy.

LaTorsha Tomlinson was pregnant with a girl. LaDainian couldn't wait to hold her, kiss her, talk to her, and spoil her. "I'm going to give that child a lot of love," he said.

FAST FACT:
The Tomlinsons were blessed with a son, Daylen, who was born in July 2010.

Then something terrible happened. In February, the young couple discovered that little McKiah would never share the huge new house LaDainian had built for their family. LaTorsha delivered the baby, but McKiah did not survive.

Now it was up to LaDainian to redirect his love for McKiah into compassion and care for his grieving wife. He would do so by leaning on a faith in Christ that he had developed before the tragedy struck.

"I was a wreck," she would say later. "LaDainian is my rock. He sacrifices his own need to grieve, pushed it to the back, to stand up and be there for me."

Is LaDainian Tomlinson a rarity? Is it unusual for macho guys—strong guys, tough guys—to be tender guys as well?

Look at what took place when Jesus faced grief head on— when Jesus' friend Lazarus died. Jesus saw the sadness in

Lazarus' sisters Mary and Martha, and He sensed his own sorrow at this event. And He responded with tears.

"Jesus wept," John 11:35 tells us. Jesus, the great creator—the One who would soon be bringing Lazarus back to life—cried.

Strong guys like LaDainian love their wives and help carry them through the toughest of times—just as the strong Man named Jesus showed compassion for Mary and Martha—and just as He gave himself for the church (Ephesians 5:25).

Are you macho, man? Show it by being strong enough to surround others with compassion and love. The best way to show that you want to honor your Savior is by being compassionate—just like He is. —DAVE BRANON

FOLLOW THROUGH

Who needs your compassion and your care right now? Is there someone who is just waiting for you to show him or her Jesus' love and concern? Why not make it a point to demonstrate your love in a tangible way today. A card. A note. A gift.

From the Playbook: Read 1 Peter 3:1–8.

TOP 25 GREAT FOOTBALL GAMES

BROWNS' BLUNDER January 17, 1988, Denver Broncos 38, Cleveland Browns 33—The Cleveland Browns were this close to going to the Super Bowl. Instead, this team will be forever remembered for a fumble by one of their best players at the most inopportune time. In the AFC Conference championship game, the Broncos led 38-31 late. But Bernie Kosar and the Browns had moved the ball near the goal line. Earnest Byner was headed for paydirt when the ball came loose, and the Broncos recovered with just over a minute left. The Broncos, not the Browns, won and went to the Super Bowl.

94. A GREAT LOSS

"Good and upright is the Lord." PSALM 25:8

Death. Tragedy. Loss.
These can make us or break us. It all depends on how we view God.

Turning tragedy into glory is not easy.

Consider what happened to Kevin Mawae. This great NFL center lost his brother in a car accident many years ago. When his brother John died, Kevin turned to the Scriptures to seek the answers he felt John had found. His brother's life had recently turned around, and he was planning to tell Kevin about it the same day he died.

FAST FACT:

Kevin Mawae, a perennial All-Pro, has served as president of the NFL Players Association.

"Two months after John's death, my wife became pregnant. This is when the questions about who God is really began. I questioned God's ability to give and then take—the miracle of birth, how I lost my closest friend, but was about to have a child of my own."

Knowing that somehow the change in his brother had been spiritual, Kevin began searching the Bible for answers. "I began going to Bible studies and reading the Bible, searching for answers. It was then that I felt God begin His work in me. I finally came to the realization that God is in control and always had been.

"Eventually, I gave my life to Christ, including my despair, questions, and my disbelief. On June 17, 1997, I got saved."

He found what John had found, he believes. "I believe he found the truth, and this caused his changed demeanor. God used John's death to bring me and my family to Christ."

Suppose instead that Kevin had become bitter with God. Suppose he refused to feel God's care. How sad that would have been.

Trust in God even in the middle of the worst times. He cares, and He wants to pour out blessings—sometimes eternal and sometimes temporal—on you. —DAVE BRANON

FOLLOW THROUGH

Has tragedy or trouble touched your life? What are you doing with it?

From the Playbook: Read Psalm 25:1–10.

TOP 25 GREAT FOOTBALL GAMES

THE ORIGINAL "HAIL MARY"   December 28, 1975, Dallas 17, Minnesota 14—According to Roger Staubach, he coined the term "Hail Mary" to describe a hopeful heave downfield by a quarterback with the intent of getting a touchdown as time runs out in a game. It was a divisional championship game pitting the Dallas Cowboys and the Minnesota Vikings. With time running out, the Vikings leading 14-10, and the ball at about the fifty-yard line, Staubach stepped back and fired the ball toward the goal line. Drew Pearson caught it and danced into the end zone with the gamewinner. Later, Staubach explained, "I closed my eyes and said a 'Hail Mary.'"

95. KIDS' STUFF

"Blessed is he who is kind to the needy."
PROVERBS 14:21
*"See that you do not look down on one of these
little ones."* MATTHEW 18:10

Former NFL running back Shaun Alexander has never forgotten his hometown of Florence, Kentucky. Even while still in the NFL, Alexander kept returning to Florence, where he visited kids in the schools. He also called the Florence High School football team's coaching staff before games on Friday nights—just to let them know he was thinking of them.

When he began playing football in high school and developed into one of the best players in the country, he didn't think of himself as special. The smiling, fun-loving kid simply realized he had "a gift from God." He had been given the gift to "play football better than a lot of people."

He was driven to use that gift, and once he established himself, he began to look for kids he could help.

Kids like Alex.

Teenager. Crohn's disease. Alex went to an NFL game in Seattle and got to meet Shaun. They swapped Bible verses. Alex started a foundation with Shaun's help. Shaun played in his golf tournament. Alex says Shaun helps him make it through when things get tough.

Alexander felt he was doing God's work. Imagine how rewarding it is to do something you know beyond a doubt is what God wants you to do.

FAST FACT:

Shaun and Valerie Alexander have four children: Heaven, Trinity, Eden, and Joseph.

Let's examine one thing that God asks us to do.

In Galatians 6:10, the apostle Paul said, "Therefore, as we have opportunity, let us do good to all people, especially to those who belong to the family of believers." This leaves no doubt. We must look for ways to help others—both in and out of the family of God.

Just as Shaun Alexander helped the kids in his old neighborhood as a way of giving back to God, we too need to find a place to take our compassion. We too need to do something that we know beyond doubt is God's work.

Please the Father. Reach out to others. Help the weak.

—DAVE BRANON

FOLLOW THROUGH

Who needs your help? Someone at church? A neighbor? Paul said, "As we have opportunity, let us do good to all people." One to ten, how are you doing at that?

From the Playbook: Read Galatians 6:9–10.

GREAT FOOTBALL GAMES

GAME FOR THE AGES   November 19, 1966, Notre Dame 10, Michigan State 10—If the 1946 ND-Army game was the Game of the Century, then this game 20 years later was a Game for the Ages. Again it was No. 1 (Notre Dame) vs. No. 2 (Michigan State). Ara Parseghian vs. Duffy Daugherty. 8-0 vs. 9-0. The teams seemed to be even in every way, and the game turned out to prove that. When the dust cleared at Spartan Stadium, the teams had battled to a 10-10 tie. The game ended in controversy when Parseghian had his team run out the clock instead of trying to move into field goal position. He settled for a tie instead of risking losing the ball back to MSU in the game's closing minutes.

96. A 280-POUND PUPPY DOG

Game Plan:
Turning our fears over to God

"In God I trust; I will not be afraid. What can man to do me?" PSALM 56:11

John Matuszak was a 6-foot-8, 280-pound football player for the Oakland Raiders. His public image was that of a havoc-wreaking, heavy-drinking, hard-hitting player who was as much a threat off the field as on. Friends, however, knew "Tooz," as he was called, as a 280-pound puppy dog just begging to be stroked.

According to *Los Angeles Times* writer Mark Heisler, John Matuszak was "beset by fears he couldn't acknowledge." As a young boy, he was ridiculed for his gawky, beanpole appearance. Two brothers died of cystic fibrosis. The image of the Tooz was a fortress he had created to hide in. But he got trapped there by his hidden fears. He died at age 38 of a massive heart attack. His body had been weakened by years of alcohol and drug abuse.

FAST FACT:

After retiring from the NFL, Matuszak became an actor, appearing in numerous movies and TV programs, including M*A*S*H and Miami Vice.

The story of King Saul bears some striking similarities. He was a monster of a man, a fighter. He was also driven by fears (1 Samuel 18:29). Because he tried to cope with them in his own strength instead of turning to the Lord for help, his life came to an untimely end (31:4).

What is going on inside of you that you are trying to hide with some kind of outer image? It may not be the facade of sports stardom or the coverup of size, but it's possible to hide behind our fears instead of turning them over to the Lord—our true source of help for things such as this.

Heavenly Father, no matter how big we may appear on the outside, sometimes we feel very small on the inside. Forgive us for putting up a false front and pretending we're strong enough to handle life on our own. Help us to trust you more. —MART DE HAAN

FOLLOW THROUGH

You can admit it here. What are you afraid of? Have you ever tried handing that fear over to God?

From the Playbook: Read 1 Samuel 18:28–19:12.

GREAT FOOTBALL GAMES

SUPER BOWL SURPRISE   January 12, 1969, New York Jets 14, Baltimore Colts 7—In 1969, most people were convinced that an American Football League team could not beat an NFL team in the newly named "Super Bowl." Joe Namath was not one of those people. He was confident his New York Jets could do it. And they did. In just the third NFL-AFL Championship Game, the merger became officially complete as Namath's team beat the favored Baltimore Colts. Namath was named the game's MVP.

97. WHAT REALLY LASTS

Game Plan:
Searching for excellence

"Those who have served well gain an excellent standing." 1 TIMOTHY 3:13

Striving for excellence is the norm in the NFL. From draft day through offseason practices and workouts through preseason training and exhibition games, teams spend innumerable hours seeking excellence. But what is the definition of excellence? Is it something quantifiable like a perfect 158 quarterback rating, or is it an undefeated season like the 1972 Miami Dolphins enjoyed?

FAST FACT:

After retiring from football, Frank Reich has been a seminary president and the pastor of a church. In 2009, he returned to the NFL as a coach with the Indianapolis Colts.

My former coach for the Buffalo Bills, Marv Levy, had this perspective: "Winning is not our goal—excellence in preparation is our goal—winning will result." It is this perspective that I favor in both defining and striving for excellence. This is more of an inside-out approach to both motivation and success. This approach levels the playing field and radically changes who is perceived as "the best."

When we use the typical "measurable" standards, the playing field is heavily tilted toward the more talented or those with the greatest resources. When the highest value is assigned to the process, however, the focus is on those who possess virtues such as diligence, faithfulness, perseverance, and integrity. This perspective does not discount the value of measurable standards, but it does put them in their proper place.

As Christians, we must be careful never to forget that God's economy is radically different from the world's. His idea of excellence is based on our relationship with God—and what lasts for eternity. Although we can and should strive for success, and we may achieve it along the way, we should not value it over success in God's eyes. Excellence for those of us who are serving Jesus is to value only what lasts for eternity—a relationship with God, an understanding of God's Word, and our relationships with people.   —FRANK REICH

FOLLOW THROUGH

How is God's view of things different from the world's in regard to what is excellent?

From the Playbook: Galatians 6:1–10.

TOP 25 GREATEST FOOTBALL GAMES

SHAKESPEARE'S SURPRISE ENDING **November 2, 1935, Notre Dame 18, Ohio State 13**—Two undefeated goliaths of college football met in Columbus, Ohio, and legendary football writer Grantland Rice was there to record the doings. With 80,000 fans looking on, the Buckeyes led 13-12 in the game's waning minutes. Andy Pilney, the quarterback of the Irish, rushed for 30 yards to put Notre Dame on OSU's 19-yard-line with just a few seconds left. Pilney was injured on the play, so William Shakespeare took over at QB (the Irish also had a player named Henry Wadsworth Longfellow), and he fired a TD pass to Wayne Milner for the win.

98. STICK TO IT

Game Plan:
Learning to keep our commitments

"No one who puts his hand to the plow and looks back is fit for service in the kingdom of God." Luke 9:62

If there is one thing former NFL lineman Chad Hennings recalls from his parents while growing up in Iowa, it was commitment.

One of Chad's earliest memories of sticking to a task was when he and his brother Todd decided to have a 4-H project—grooming steers for competition. The boys had to feed them twice a day, halter-train them, groom them, make sure their hair was cut and combed, and train them to walk properly in preparation for showings. It was a huge undertaking. Both Todd and Chad were successful. One of their steers became a Grand Champion.

FAST FACT:

In 1996, Dave Branon assisted Chad with his autobiography It Takes Commitment. *Hennings wrote a second book,* Rules of Engagement, *which was published after he retired from the NFL.*

Chad's parents continued to influence him to stick to his tasks in life—whether it was sticking with a musical instrument once he got started or staying with a sport no matter how tough or unenjoyable it might become. He learned, he says, "Running from my fears would never make them go away. Only when I faced my fears could I conquer them."

No wonder Chad could sail through his years at the Air Force Academy, become an Air Force pilot, and enjoy an outstanding career with the Dallas Cowboys.

In our lives as Christians, what is our goal? If it is to bring glory to God through our lives (which is the right answer), then we must face that task with a commitment that mirrors Jacob's commitment to Laban.

Another vital task God asks us to do is to love our neighbors as ourselves. This is where commitment really gets tested. Dealing with people can lead to frustrations that make us want to avoid those who cause us trouble. But if we are truly dedicated to service for others as a way of honoring God, we stay committed to showing Christlike love and Spirit-led compassion.

And we'll stick with the task until it gets done.

—DAVE BRANON

FOLLOW THROUGH

In what area do you feel that you struggle with commitment—where you feel like quitting because it's tough? How can Abraham's example and God's love for you keep you from giving up?

From the Playbook: Read Genesis 22:1–19.

GREAT FOOTBALL GAMES

THE BUSH PUSH   **October 15, 2005, USC 34, Notre Dame 31**—The Trojans came into South Bend ranked No. 1 in the country, and the Irish were 4-1. It appeared that Charlie Weis had righted the ship. The teams battled evenly throughout the game, and with less than two minutes left, Brady Quinn scored to give Notre Dame a 31-28 lead. Matt Leinart led the Trojans back down the field. With the final seconds ticking away, Leinart tried to score from the one, but the ball squirted out of bounds. USC had one more play. Leinart tried a QB sneak, and with Reggie Bush pushing him from behind, he crossed the line for the win.

99. DECISIONS, DECISIONS

Game Plan:
Developing biblical decision-making

"In all your ways acknowledge him, and he will make your paths straight." PROVERBS 3:6

The first Wednesday in February has become a national sports holiday—it's National Signing Day! This is the day high school football stars make a decision that will have a significant impact on the rest of their lives. It's the day high school stars sign their letter of intent and announce their plans to attend the collegiate football powerhouse of their choice.

How does a young athlete go about making a choice of that magnitude? For many it's based on the coaching staff; for others, the school's football tradition; and for still others, it's the opportunity to play—sooner rather than later.

FAST FACT:

The fans of many high-profile schools like LSU, Florida State, and Tennessee host National Signing Day parties.

For any Christ-follower, star athlete or otherwise, the decision-making process should always begin with one primary tool: The Bible. (Other tools such as listening to the Holy Spirit, discussing things with Christian friends and leaders, and committing the matter to personal prayer are also critical.)

The Bible is God's Word. It is truth. You can trust it as God's revelation of himself to man. Because it is trustworthy, we can and should use it as a reliable guide for life's biggest and most crucial decisions.

In the Scriptures, God gives clear guidance on what to do— and what not to do. The Ten Commandments in the Old Testament and Jesus' Sermon on the Mount in the New Testament are prime examples of God's clear direction to His people.

In Romans 12:2, the apostle Paul exhorts believers in pursuing God's truth for direction that leads to discernment. "Do not conform any longer to the pattern of this world, but be transformed by the renewing of your mind. Then you will be able to test and approve what God's will is—his good, pleasing and perfect will."

Looking to make the right decision? Seeking God's will in your situation? Begin by pursuing God's guidance found in His Word.   —ROB BENTZ

FOLLOW THROUGH

God's Word does not give detailed answers to your specific, personal questions. But it does provide you with clear guidelines that can help you navigate your specific situation or decision.

From the Playbook: Read and memorize Proverbs 3:5–6.

TOP 25 GREAT FOOTBALL GAMES

GREAT SCOTT! **November 8, 1980, Georgia 26, Florida 21—** Herschel Walker was supposed to be the big story in this game. Georgia's remarkable running back was a joy to behold. But in the end, it was a guy named Lindsay Scott who stole the spotlight. Georgia trailed Florida 21-20 in the closing minutes. Buck Belue was in trouble. Third and 10 on his own seven with about a minute left. Belue dropped back into his own end zone, frantically searching for a receiver. Suddenly Scott broke open on the 25. Belue fired the ball to him, and he was off to the races. Lindsay Scott caught the ball and scampered for a 93-yard touchdown and kept Georgia's national title hopes alive.

100. WE ARE FAMILY

Game Plan:
Making family a priority

"Unless the Lord builds the house, its builders labor in vain." PSALM 127:1

When a father has his priorities right—whether he's the head coach of a Top 10 football team or a third-grade teacher at the local elementary school—things will go pretty well in the family.

Longtime University of Georgia coach Mark Richt is that kind of guy. He's a got-priorities-right kind of dad. His family knows he's there for them first. His football team has his attention, but his family has his heart.

FAST FACT:

In his first nine years as head coach at Georgia, Richt and his teams won at least nine games in seven of those years. They won 77 percent of their games from 2001 through 2009.

In the late 1990s Mark and Kathryn Richt had heard about a couple of kids who lived in an orphanage in Ukraine, and they began to pray for them. Then the family decided that prayer was not enough. They wanted to go get Zack and Anya, and bring them into their home.

So Mark and Katharyn left for Ukraine to pick up Zack and Anya. It was not easy. Katharyn had to stay in the country for 31 days, and Mark was there for 8 days. Finally, in July that year, Jon and David had new siblings.

The Richts had their work cut out for them.

"It took the children time to learn the ropes, to learn the language," Coach Richt told *Sports Spectrum* magazine. "There were a lot of barriers that had to be established and lots of trust and love that had to be developed."

In Psalm 128 we read about a person who walks in the ways of God, who eats the fruit of his labor. Because he fears the Lord—and consequently cares properly for his family—he is blessed.

That means that God's smile of approval is on him. That's the kind of guy Mark Richt shows us how to be.

Being a parent has no guarantees. However, it is essential for moms and dads to fear the Lord and walk in His way if they expect His blessing.

What have you done today to put your family's priorities in the order you think God would have you put them?

—DAVE BRANON

FOLLOW THROUGH

Is there any difference between what you say are your top priorities and what you actually demonstrate them to be? If God is a priority, for instance, how would "Time with God" fit on a chart for time spent? Same with other elements of life.

From the Playbook: Read Psalm 127 and 128.

TOP 25 GREAT FOOTBALL GAMES

WIDE RIGHT   January 27, 1991, New York Giants 20, Buffalo Bills 19—Imagine what would have happened if Scott Norwood's last-second, 47-yard kick in Super Bowl XXV had drifted a few feet left and had sneaked inside the uprights. Imagine if instead of losing 20-19, the Buffalo Bills would have defeated the New York Giants 22-20. Imagine if Norwood had become a Buffalo hero. Imagine if the Bills then rode the momentum of the win to capture—not lose—the next three Super Bowls. What a difference a few feet make to a team and to a city.

KEY VERSE LIST

Verse	Article Number	Title
HOCKEY		
Genesis 50:20	10	Three Ordinary Guys
Exodus 3:2	12	How Holly Met Bob
I Samuel 16:7	5	"Is That a Girl Playing Hockey?"
Psalm 37:4	7	From Nightmare to Dream
Psalm 111:2	4	A Wilderness Adventure
Mark 5:22	6	More Important Than the Cup!
Luke 12:4	11	Afraid?
John 3:3	18	Turned Away
Acts 4:12	15	"Dear Dominic"
Romans 8:28	14	In the Middle of a Struggle
I Corinthians 11:24	22	Create a Monument
I Corinthians 12:12	1	Hanging Out With Gretzky
I Corinthians 12:19–20	21	We're All Goalies
2 Corinthians 5:9	8	The Greatest Goal
2 Corinthians 12:9	16	Think Fast!
Ephesians 4:15	19	Captain Coyote
Ephesians 4:32	20	Remarkable Forgiveness
Ephesians 6:13	3	My Two Front Teeth
Philippians 3:8	9	A Temporary Job
I Timothy 4:12	17	Too Young?
I Timothy 4:15	24	The Apprentice
Titus 2:12	25	Keep an Eye on Him!
Hebrews 9:27	2	Hockey, Pistol Pete, and Heaven
James 1:12	23	Zach and the Kid
I Peter 1:4–5	13	Got You Covered
BASKETBALL		
I Samuel 16:7	44	Getting Fit
Psalm 71:5	42	J Will's Deferred Dream
Psalm 111:10	26	Seeking Wisdom and Understanding
Proverbs 16:9	41	Setting Up Some Expectations
Ecclesiastes 2:23	36	Not Enough
Ecclesiastes 4:12	30	Five Superstars

Matthew 16:26	29	Pistol Pete's Search
Mark 14:9	48	Jimmy Chitwood's Jumper
John 4:14	46	Lessons from the Waterboys
Romans 3:22–23	31	Stand Tall
Romans 8:1	40	The Great Jimmy V.
Romans 8:17	47	No Pain, No Gain
Romans 12:18	35	Cooler Heads
I Corinthians 1:10	33	The Bond of Basketball—and Beyond
I Corinthians 3:14	45	The Best Legacy
I Corinthians 12:20	37	Steve Nash's Ego
Philippians 2:4	38	Driving a Different Lane
Philippians 4:8	32	What's Your Focal Point?
I Timothy 1:18	27	Not-so-Fundamental
I Timothy 4:12	50	Be an Example
Titus 1.9	39	Original Rules for Sale
James 1:3	34	Sign Me Up!
2 Peter 3:8	49	Game-clock Math
3 John 11	43	Playing Like the Pistol
Revelation 12:10	28	The Shot That Made March Mad

BASEBALL

Exodus 34:21	58	Take Time to Rest
I Kings 15:11	59	What Big Mac Lacks
Psalm 42:5	64	In a Slump?
Proverbs 16:31	51	The Legacy of Ernie Harwell
Proverbs 24:16	55	My Awful Week
Daniel 1:8	62	A Legacy of Resilience
Micah 7:18	67	Forgive and Remember
Matthew 5:5	54	What Will the Outcome Be?
Luke 3:22	66	A Proud Father
Luke 9:23	68	Cutting Out Shortcuts
Romans 5:8	70	What Pete Rose Can't Get
I Corinthians 4:5	52	Take Me Out to the Ball Game
I Corinthians 6:20	60	Extra Boost?
I Corinthians 11:1	72	The Power of Example
Philippians 2:14	63	The Complain Game
Philippians 3:12	75	Sweeney's Surrender
Titus 3:7	53	Are You Optimistic?
Hebrews 10:10	65	Curses!

Hebrews 11:1	57	Moses, Hope, and the Chicago Cubs
James 2:13	71	Cutting Some Slack
James 4:17	74	Do the Right Thing
I Peter 3:15	73	Come On, Ump!
I Peter 4:10	69	What My Player Can Do
I John 1:7	56	As If It Never Happened
3 John 11	61	Don't Imitate Him

FOOTBALL

I Chronicles 28:9	81	He Kept Going and Going . . .
Psalm 25:8	94	A Great Loss
Psalm 39:7	84	Lasting Satisfaction?
Psalm 56:11	96	A 280-Pound Puppy Dog
Psalm 100:2	77	You Do What on Sunday?
Psalm 127:1	100	We Are Family
Proverbs 3:6	99	Decisions, Decisions
Proverbs 14:21	95	Kids' Stuff
Proverbs 16:18	92	Leon's Lapse
Proverbs 27:2	86	The Right Role Model
Daniel 3:12	78	One Single Fan
Matthew 4:17	89	A Fresh Start
Matthew 7:14	82	Going the Right Way?
Matthew 18:20	95	Kids' Stuff
Mark 16:15	76	You're Not Tim Tebow!
Luke 9:62	98	Stick to It
I Corinthians 9:12	88	Take One for the Team
I Corinthians 16:13	87	Be Like Mike . . . Brown
Galatians 6:2	93	Tender Macho Man
Galatians 6:10	80	Why Walk Away?
Ephesians 5:15–16	83	Say No to Immorality
Colossians 3:2	79	Only Way to Turn
I Thessalonians 5:22	91	Double Coverage Trouble
I Timothy 3:13	97	What Really Lasts
2 Timothy 1:6	85	Encouragement and Instruction
I Peter 5:5	90	A Humbling Experience

SPORTS PEOPLE

Brief biographical notes about the sports people who contributed articles to Power Up! All-Star Edition.

RON BROWN A longtime coach for the Nebraska Cornhuskers, Brown has also been extremely involved with the Fellowship of Christian Athletes and a Nebraska-based organization called Mission Nebraska. He has spent more than two decades coaching receivers at Nebraska.

TIM CASH A stint in the minor leagues with the Houston Astros and Los Angeles Dodgers organizations prepared Tim for his life work of discipling major league baseball players through Unlimited Potential, Inc. Cash lives in the Atlanta area, where he worked for many years as the chaplain for the Atlanta Braves. He is now a pastor in the Atlanta area.

SHANNA CROSSLEY After a remarkable high school career at Wawasee High School in Syracuse, Indiana, Shanna went to the University of Tennessee where she played for legendary coach Pat Summitt. In 2006, she began her WNBA career. She has played for the San Antonio Stars and the Tulsa Shock.

SHANE DOAN As the only holdover from the Winnipeg Jets, Doan became the captain of the Phoenix Coyotes in 2003. On the international hockey scene, Doan has won both gold and silver medals for Canada. He grew up on a ranch that doubles as a Christian camp in Alberta. He is related through marriage to Catriona Le May Doan, who has won three Olympic gold medals for Canada.

DAVID FISHER For many years, David Fisher ministered to professional hockey players through the auspices of Hockey Ministries

International (HMI). He also served as chaplain for the Toronto Blue Jays for 29 seasons. Fisher also maintains contact with many pro athletes through letters and other communications to encourage them spiritually.

MIKE GARTNER A member of the Hockey Hall of Fame, Gartner scored 1,335 points in his long NHL career. After one year in the World Hockey Association, Gartner played 22 NHL seasons for the Washington Capitals, the Minnesota North Stars, the New York Rangers, the Toronto Maple Leafs, and the Phoenix Coyotes. For a time after his career ended, he served with the NHL Players Association.

DEB PATTERSON Twenty-win seasons became commonplace for Deb Patterson during her tenure as women's basketball coach at Kansas State. Named the Big 12 Coach of the Year on multiple occasions, Patterson led her 2005 team to a WNIT championship. Oddly, while Patterson was a college field hockey player, she never played basketball in college.

FRANK REICH Frank Reich was the backup quarterback to Jim Kelly in Buffalo during the Super Bowl years. In 1995, the Carolina Panthers picked him in the expansion draft, and he went on to play also for the New York Jets and the Detroit Lions. His strong Christian faith led him to pursue ministry after his NFL career ended, including working with a Christian Web site for a time, then becoming both a pastor and a seminary president. He later returned to the NFL as a coach.

MATT STOVER When Matt Stover kicked for the Indianapolis Colts in Super Bowl XLIV, he became the oldest player (42 years, 11 days) to appear in a Super Bowl game. Stover was a member of a Super Bowl-winning team in 2001 when the Baltimore Ravens won SB XXXV. During his career, Stover scored more than 2,000 points, putting him among the Top 5 scorers in league history.

POWER UP WRITERS

Brief biographical notes about the writers who contributed articles to Power Up! All-Star Edition.

JEFF ARNOLD Jeff Arnold once endured an NFL media mini camp as part of his duties covering the Tennessee Titans. When his dream career as a NFL tight end didn't pan out, he returned his focus to reporting. Now a sports reporter with AnnArbor.com, Arnold spends more time around the college game, working as part of AnnArbor.com's Michigan football coverage team, in addition to serving as the site's Michigan hockey beat writer.

ROB BENTZ After working for several years for *Sports Spectrum* magazine and radio right out of college, Rob left RBC Ministries to attend Reformed Theological Seminary in Orlando, where he received a master's degree in ministry. He is now serving as pastor of small groups at Woodmen Valley Chapel in Colorado Springs, Colorado.

DAVE BRANON For 18 years, Dave was managing editor of *Sports Spectrum* magazine. Currently, he is an editor for Discovery House Publishers and RBC Ministries. He is a regular contributing writer for *Our Daily Bread*. Over the years, he has written a number of books for a variety of publishers. His latest book is *Beyond the Valley*, published in 2010 by Discovery House Publishers.

BILL CROWDER After playing college soccer at Liberty University, Crowder spent a long time as a pastor. Currently, he works at RBC Ministries as an associate teacher, traveling worldwide in a Bible conference ministry. He also serves as chaplain for the *Sports Spectrum* radio program of RBC, and he has written several books published by Discovery House Publishers.

JOSH COOLEY A 17-year sportswriting veteran, Josh works full-time as the children's ministry administrator at his church in Gaithersburg, Maryland. He has written numerous articles for *Sports Spectrum* magazine, including profiles of Tim Tebow, Colt McCoy, Jim Zorn, and Sam Bradford.

DAN DEAL After working as a radio producer and occasional host of *Sports Spectrum* radio at RBC Ministries for several years, Deal left to work on the staff of Ada Bible Church in Ada, Michigan, as director of small group training and resources.

MART DE HAAN Mart is president of RBC Ministries. His grandfather, Dr. M. R. De Haan, founded RBC in 1938. Mart has written several books, including *Been Thinking About,* a publication of Discovery House Publishers.

TOM FELTEN Another former *Sports Spectrum* magazine person—Tom was manager of *SS* radio and magazine for several years—he now is managing editor of *Our Daily Journey,* one of the devotional guides produced by RBC Ministries. The online version of *ODJ* can be read at www.ourdailyjourney.org.

TIM GUSTAFSON When not serving in the US Navy Reserves, Tim works at RBC Ministries, where he is former editor of *Our Daily Bread* and currently Director of Print Ministries. He and his wife, Leisa, have eight children, just a few of whom have inherited Tim's love for the Detroit Tigers. Gustafson has served the Navy overseas in Japan and the Philippines.

BRIAN HETTINGA The host and producer of the weekly radio program *Discover the Word,* an outreach of RBC Ministries, Hettinga played small college basketball before trading in his Chuck Taylors for a microphone. Despite the passage of time and a battle with cancer, Brian still has one of the best-looking jump shots around.

VICTOR LEE A longtime beat writer covering major league baseball and later a regular writer for *Sports Spectrum* magazine, Lee left the world of fulltime journalism to become a pastor. He serves as minister of single adults and evangelism at a church in Knoxville, while still writing sports articles when he can find the time.

JEFF OLSON When he has to put down his fishing gear or his hunting rifle and come inside, Jeff can be coaxed back to his desk at RBC Ministries, where he is a biblical counselor. Olson has written several booklets for the RBC Discovery Series Bible studies. Besides his work with RBC, Olson has a private counseling practice and enjoys speaking at men's retreats.

MOLLY RAMSEYER As a college student, Molly worked with *Sports Spectrum* magazine as an intern. She did such a good job she was offered the chance to write for the magazine later. After college, she began working with Youth for Christ on the local level. Currently, she is national director of camping for Youth for Christ. She lives in Englewood, California, with her husband, Dave.

ROXANNE ROBBINS After hobnobbing with the influential and famous in Washington D. C. for several years in positions relating to public relations, Roxanne left it all behind to go to Uganda to live among kids with nothing. A longtime writer for *Sports Spectrum*, she knows athletes up-close and personal, but she has discovered the importance of the oft-neglected little guys and girls who cherish someone who cares for them. While in Africa, Roxanne adopted a little boy.

NOTE TO THE READER

The publisher invites you to share your response to the message of this book by writing Discovery House Publishers, P.O. Box 3566, Grand Rapids, MI 49501, U.S.A. For information about other Discovery House books, music, videos, or DVDs, contact us at the same address or call 1-800-653-8333. Find us on the Internet at http://www.dhp.org/ or send e-mail to books@dhp.org.